"If a mature religion is one that can laugh at itself, then Mormonism is growing up. . . . Bigelow and his staff of *Sugar Beet* writers, whose identities are hidden behind ultra-Mormon pseudonyms, ferret out the delicious humor tucked away in Mormonism's quirkiest doctrines and cultural extremes. . . . Readers will find the *Enquirer* a tie-loosening, glue gun melting pleasure—and an excellent Christmas gift for friends and family."

—*Publishers Weekly*

THE MORMON TABERNACLE
ENQUIRER

Written by Paul Allen, Paul Browning, Christopher Kimball Bigelow,
Stephen Carter, Amy Chamberlain, Chris Giauque, Todd Robert Petersen,
Eric Samuelsen, Kathy Tyner, Holly Welker, and others

Edited and compiled by Christopher Kimball Bigelow

PINCE-NEZ PRESS

Printed in the U.S.A.

ISBN 10: 1-930074-17-4
ISBN 13: 978-1-930074-17-0
LCCN: 2006930481

Cover design, page design and layout: Paul Browning

This book uses invented names in all stories, except notable public figures who are the subjects of satire. Any other use of real names is accidental and coincidental.

Published by:
Pince-Nez Press
www.pince-nez.com

CONTENTS

Chapter 1:

Who Are These Children Coming Down?

Back in the 1970s, Mormons all over the world thrilled to the sounds of the musical smash hit *Saturday's Warrior*, which taught us that spirit children are eagerly awaiting their turn to help build the kingdom during these last days. The title song asked, *"Who are these children coming down, like gentle rain from darkened skies?"*

While we haven't ever actually been hit by a heaven-sent newborn during a rainstorm, this is a question the crack reporters at *The Mormon Tabernacle Enquirer* take quite seriously. This chapter collects our reportage on Mormons aged negative infinity to eighteen in mortal years.

From the recent discovery that Cheerios in fact make children more restless during church to the teenaged priest who set a new record for flubbing the sacrament prayer the most times, these reports paint a compelling collective portrait of the rising generation—you know, the ones *"with glory trailing from their feet as they come and endless promise in their eyes."*

Premortal World Rocked by Family-Swapping Scandal

By M. Spencer Pratt

PREMORTAL WORLD—Authorities here are investigating reports of a practice that has scandalized the normally placid spirits awaiting birth. According to the Secretary of Family Assignments, two spirits who had been scheduled to be born as Alma Nelson and Bernard Carter, respectively, allegedly arranged to switch birth families just days before their imminent births.

During an exclusive interview, the original Alma admitted to the trade and explained his reasoning. "See, I knew I was going to be born into an LDS family, which I thought was great, originally. But now my birth is close enough that I can actually observe the other Nelsons, and I have to say they leave much to be desired. Mainly, they're—well, how do I put this? They're really Mormon. I mean, they have family home evening three times a week, they live in Magna, they have family scripture study for like an hour a day, they make the kids go to every single ward activity there is ... I mean, they don't even have a TV! Let alone a Playstation 2. Plus, I'd be baby number ten out of a scheduled twelve. You think I'd be getting my own car in high school? I don't. So, yeah, I knew I'd go nuts if I were born into that family."

"When we got talking," said the original Bernard, "I suddenly realized that we might be able to help each other. I'd been watching my future family too, and while they were well off, loving, and doted on my sister, they lacked a spiritual anchor. I was worried about my ability to find my way back home if I were born into such a secular situation. After all, nothing will be more important to me down there

than my spiritual well-being. I jumped at the chance to be born under the covenant into the one true church."

"Yeah, you should see their place," added pre-Alma. "It's awesome! They've got a big-screen TV, a pool, and not just a PS2 but an XBox too! And Daddy Carter drives a Jag! I figure I can always find some missionaries later in life, after I've had some fun. Or, jeez, if worse came to worst, there are missionaries in spirit prison. I'd make it eventually. What's the big deal?"

The authorities in charge of such matters aren't so nonchalant. "I'm glad we caught this in time," said a spokes-spirit. "You can't imagine the recordkeeping nightmare a switch like this would have caused. Not to mention little things like, oh, foreordination and fulfillment of prophecies. Plus, we just realized today that the Nelsons are white, while the Carters are black. You can't switch races, for crying out loud!"

When informed that they would not be allowed to switch, pre-Bernard stated his acceptance. "I'm sure they know best. I'll just have to take the hard way back home," he said. Pre-Alma, on the other hand, was less than enthusiastic. "Didn't I fight in the war in heaven for the side that favored free agency? So much for that, I guess."

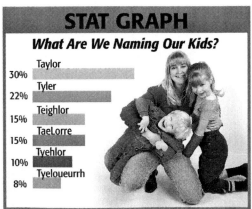

STAT GRAPH
What Are We Naming Our Kids?

Taylor	30%
Tyler	22%
Teighlor	15%
TaeLorre	15%
Tyehlor	10%
Tyeloueurrh	8%

Study Shows Cheerios May Cause Restlessness and Crying
By Terrill W. Cannon &
M. Spencer Pratt

LAWRENCE, KS—When Mormon babies fuss during church, Cheerios are the number-one snack parents use to quiet them down. However, researchers at the University of Kansas's Department of Molecular, Cellular, and Developmental Biology have discovered that this breakfast cereal can cause serious digestion problems in children.

The key discovery was that wheat gluten undergoes a unique transformation during the rolling and extruding segments of the Cheerios manufacturing process. The gluten protein is rearranged into a new functional molecule that has unexpected effects on the immature digestive systems of children as old as three years. "It's similar to the creation of prions in mad cow disease," said lead researcher Dr. S.S. Moorty.

Although the effects of the new protein are not yet fully understood, it is clear that it activates at least two important metabolic pathways, one resulting in increased adrenaline production and the other activating the enzyme COX-1, a pain signaler. "We have shown that the increased adrenaline is directly correlated to an average 78% increase in the child's fuss index, while the COX-1 activity results in a 53% increase in pain-related vocalizations, or crying," explained Moorty.

"I don't know what we can give her now. She just spits Rice Chex on the floor."

Parents with young children are bewildered. Katrina Leaventhal-Young, a mother from Provo, Utah, has been feeding her daughter, Mackenzie, Cheerios since she came off breast milk. "We'd even bring them with us to church," she said. "But things are all beginning to make sense now. On Sundays Mackenzie would be fine all morning, but once the opening hymn was over, she'd be fussy and squirmy. I thought she was hungry, so I'd open a little bag of Cheerios and give her one—oh, this is terrible." After composing herself, Leaventhal-Young added, "I thought we were helping. I don't know what we can give her now. She just spits Rice Chex on the floor."

General Mills is considering a recall of the cereal, at least in Utah and southeast Idaho.

Cereal and Cheddar Fish Miracle Occurs in Nursery
By Teancum Zenos Smoot IV

CAMBRIDGE, MA—When the treat bucket failed to arrive at the Cambridge Second Ward nursery last Sunday morning, nursery worker Helen Stascbury knew they needed a miracle. "When fifteen toddlers are hungry, you don't want to be nearby," she said.

As the children started chewing on building blocks and sucking on toy dinosaur heads, the nursery workers gathered and prayed. Acting on inspiration, the workers combed the cupboards and storage closets for food remnants. Finding only a few cheddar fish crackers and a small box of raisins, the workers knew they needed more.

Through contributions from Sunday school, priesthood, and Relief Society classes, the women were able to gather a small feast for the hungry children, including a box of Tic Tacs, three suckers, a tin of Altoids, and a Tupperware container full of week-old Cheerios.

"Our greatest blessing came when we got down on our knees and crawled under the chapel benches. Dry cereal was spread beneath them like manna," said nursery worker Barbara Hicks. ▶

But then, during cleanup, the greatest miracle occurred. "I swear we swept at least twelve treat bucketsful of fish crackers, Cheerios, and raisins off the floor," said Stasebury.

"We could only offer a little bit," Hicks said through her tears, "but through the childlike faith of the children, everyone was fed, and look how much was left over."

Nursery-Aged Members Counseled to Wear Appropriate Clothing
By Kylee-Ashlee Cannon Christiansen

PROVO, UT—In a special Utah area nursery meeting held last Wednesday, the state's one-and-a-half to three-year-olds were asked to wear more modest clothing. Elder Clark H. Weimar of the Nineteenth Quorum of the Seventy spoke to an audience of over one thousand toddlers and warned them of the dangers of immodest clothing.

"You children are the future of the church," he said, "and it's never too young for you to start preparing for the temple." He warned against the evils of "cute little sundresses that show too much bare arm" and onesies that are "form-fitting enough to show diaper outlines."

"Remember that younger church members will be looking to you to set a good example," Weimar explained. He acknowledged that, while it's tempting to dress in clothes that snap up the legs to facilitate diaper changes, "such styles are not in keeping with temple standards and must be shunned at all costs."

Because stores like Gymboree and Baby Gap are pushing frilly tank tops and too-short shorts, Elder Weimar stressed the importance of avoiding such places. "You young members should not give in to the pressure of dressing like more worldly infants," he said. "If you can't find clothing modest enough, consider learning how to make your own."

He ended his fireside by reminding the children that if they start dressing in garment-worthy clothes now, they will not have to make any drastic changes to their wardrobes when they go to the temple. "I urge you to get in the habit now of covering up your arms and legs," he said. "Although adorable and chubby, your bare limbs could cause your peers to have inappropriate thoughts."

Elder Weimar's talk was received with tears, babbling, and Cheerio-crunching.

New Meetinghouses to Include Primary Playplace
By Kylee-Ashlee Cannon Christiansen

SALT LAKE CITY—In a move that Primary leaders everywhere are cheering, the Church Building Committee has unveiled a new chapel plan featuring a two-story Playplace attached to the Primary room.

The addition was inspired by a Logan stake Primary president's visit to an area McDonald's. "One look at that indoor Playland, and I knew I'd found the answer to our reverence problems," said President Sandra McClure. She sent her idea to church headquarters, where it was greeted with enthusiasm.

Playlands have already been built as a pilot project in several stakes, and all the leaders are calling it a success. The design includes a Manna Pit full of round, soft plastic balls; a twenty-foot-high Jacob's Ladder that leads to a platform called the Rameumptom; and a slide called the Slippery Slope of Sin. During Primary, children are rotated through the structure by age group for fifteen-minute intervals.

"With these scriptural names, we figure kids will get more out of Primary," said President McClure. "And we're building brand loyalty that will keep them coming back to church with their own children one day."

Little Cloud Demands More Exposure
By Teancum Zenos Smoot IV

SALT LAKE CITY—Generous anthropomorphic Primary song character Little Cloud is tired of being upstaged by Little Stream and is threatening legal action.

Cloud, who appears in the second verse of "Give Said the Little Stream," says Stream has violated a number of clauses in their contract.

"Before I ever agreed to this Primary song business, I made it contractually clear that we were to have equal time in the song. But then, at the last minute, Mr. Stream becomes the title of the song and the first verse. I ask you, is that equal face time?"

A recent poll of Primary children shows that Cloud's grievances may have some substance. Out of a hundred surveys, fifty showed that the child had not even heard of Cloud. However, twenty-five percent of the surveys were disqualified because they were either not marked clearly or were marked in something other than crayon. Another five percent were defaced with drawings of little human figures with large eyes and hands.

Cloud says that the only way for Stream to settle the matter out of court is to put Cloud into the title and first verse of the song in the next edition of the Primary Children's Songbook.

"I think we owe it to our Primary children to think about me as a metaphor for generosity more often than they do," said Cloud, who claims that, droplet for droplet, it has given just as much as Stream. "In fact, Little Stream wouldn't have a whole heck of a lot to give if it weren't for me."

Lost Child Found by Non-Mormon Gentile

By Teancum Zenos Smoot IV

LOGAN, UT—Tears of joy abounded as six-year-old LDS girl McKayla Smith was reunited with her mother and father Thursday evening. Her safe return from the forest abutting Mountain View Campground was made possible by the dedicated efforts of non-LDS man Gary Cottam, who found the girl sitting under a tree at about 10:46 p.m., crying over a sprained ankle.

When McKayla was first reported lost, Cottam, who is not a member of the LDS Church, joined an ad hoc volunteer search and rescue squad. The night was cold and rainy, but, gathering strength from something besides the true gospel, Cottam pressed on through thick foliage, searching for the lost girl.

"It was quite a trial," said Cottam, ironically using a word many Mormons also employ when describing difficult situations. "Once I thought I was lost myself, but I prayed and felt led by an unseen force to a familiar place," said the unbaptized man, showing that sometimes heaven even answers the prayers of sheep who still wander in darkness and sin.

Led by a power other than the constant companionship of the Holy Ghost, Cottam says that he walked almost straight to the lost little girl after asking God, whose true nature Cottam does not yet understand, for help.

"I just followed where my heart told me to go, and suddenly there she was. It really strengthened my faith in God's love," said Cottam, surprisingly sounding not unlike a testimony bearer at an LDS fast and testimony meeting, which he has never attended, preferring to go to another church that is an abomination before God.

Heroically, Cottam wrapped young McKayla in his own jacket and, like Jesus, whose church Cottam has not yet joined, comforted her.

"She was crying about her ankle and didn't think she could walk home," Cottam remembered, "so we said a prayer together asking God to help her feel better. And it seemed to work." Cottam shed a tear at this memory, probably feeling the Spirit for the first time in his joyless, gospel-bereft existence.

After carrying the girl to safety, Cottam tried to slip out of the picture quietly, unknowingly applying the principle of humility taught in the church, but not before Robert and Celia Smith gave him a righteous, spirit-filled shower of gratitude.

"He was such a nice man, even though he's not a member," said Celia. "He's definitely ripe for baptism," she added with a knowing wink.

"And after he joins the church, he'll make a fine example for our children," Robert agreed.

Existence of Nine Children Suggests "Intimate Relations" Between Mom, Dad

by Teancum Zenos Smoot IV

POCATELLO, ID—Until recently, the children of Carl and Anita Jones never suspected their parents of having engaged in any activities of a "gross and oogie" nature. However, fourteen-year-old daughter Jennifer recently encountered certain biological facts that have raised new suspicions. The shocked Jennifer announced her findings at a recent secret meeting with her siblings.

"I can't believe it! I just won't believe it," said a tearful Jennifer, who has always looked up to her mother, who is also her Young Women president. "All those lessons about the edelweiss, that perfect flower far from the road that was never sullied. All those warnings about parking with boys in dark places. And to think that she—" Jennifer burst into tears.

There is every possibility the Joneses are continuing in their secret combinations even to this day.

"I just—eww, I can't even think about it. Just—just go away, it's sick," said thirteen-year-old Sean Jones, whose bedroom is adjacent to his parents'.

The news has also reached Bradford Jones, who is serving a mission in Amsterdam. "I hope Mom and Dad find the strength to repent of their transgressions," wrote Elder Bradford in a secret communication with his siblings. "I can only pray that they entered into this unsavory state as few times as possible, so that their punishment will not be too harsh."

Despite the mountains of evidence pointing toward Mommy and Daddy's secret propensities, they continue to act as if nothing untoward has occurred. The children speculate that there is every possibility the Joneses are continuing in their secret combinations even to this day.

"I just hope the neighbors don't find out," said nine-year-old Susie. "I'd just die."

Jennifer attempted to console her younger sister, telling her that Mommy and Daddy have shown no outward signs of their hidden acts. She reported that Daddy magnifies his calling as ward executive secretary, always showing up with a white shirt and tie and compiling impeccable minutes during bishopric meetings. He also sings in the ward choir, owns a Ford, and votes Republican.

In addition, Jennifer lauded Mommy's almost impenetrable façade, baking cakes for ward activities, maintaining a perfect coiffure, and boasting a lifetime ninety-eight-percent visiting teaching record.

SNAPSHOT

What phrases do you **not** *want to hear in a patriarchal blessing?*

Morning of the third resurrection

Some seriously bad mojo

Flesh-eating

Gender confusion

Outer darkness

Lazy, shiftless rat-bastard

Impalement

Unfortunate series of events

The tribe and lineage of Michael Jackson

Male Impersonators Outed at Father-Son Activity
By Molly Thatcher Woodruff

LOGAN, UT—The annual Cache Valley Stake father-son outing was nearly cancelled on its second day last weekend when a case of hidden identity was discovered.

Trouble erupted when Brother Hyrum G. Thatcher was found to have smuggled two of his daughters dressed in T-shirts and pants, with their hair stuffed into baseball caps, into the traditionally all-male event.

Thatcher insisted on trying to explain himself. "You gotta understand, I got five girls. I tried to convince my wife that maybe she could feel a little masculine spirit who wanted to come to our family too, but she said no, the factory's closed. I know I shouldn't have done this, but I couldn't stand to miss the fun another year. I never knew them fellas took this all so seriously."

The crowd became aware of the girls' presence when one of them won a series of foot races and she and her sister threw off their baseball caps in triumph. "That's when all H-E-double-toothpick broke loose," Thatcher said.

"Next thing you know, they'll want the priesthood."

An angry crowd quickly gathered, and Thatcher's daughters stood in front of their father and acted as shields with their fists cocked, ready to defend him. Thatcher's bishop dispersed the mob, but he told Thatcher to report to his office the next day. "This could give the gals dangerous ideas. Next thing you know, they'll want the priesthood."

Priest Repeats Sacrament Prayer Seven Times, Breaks Ward Record
By LeVoy Mann

AMERICAN FORK, UT—During last Sunday's sacrament service at the East Bay Second Ward, sixteen-year-old Sean Brown broke the long-standing record for most repeats of the sacramental prayer. A joyous cheer followed the bishop's official approval of Brown's seventh consecutive blessing of the bread.

"I was worried there," Brown said, "because I was getting hoarse after about the fourth time." Brown's name will be inscribed on a commemorative plaque that will hang in the foyer of the Freedom Stake Center.

Special Awards Slated for Wakeful Seminary Students
By Teancum Zenos Smoot IV

SALT LAKE CITY—This year early-morning seminaries will be handing out medals of achievement and valor to students who demonstrate a high degree of wakefulness. The award, which will be called the "Order of the Watchmen," will be given to graduating seniors who, in addition to attending the required number of classes, manage to stay awake for more than eighty-five percent of them.

CES spokesman L. Robert Zimmerman says that they don't expect to give out many of the awards at first, "but we hope to separate the sheep from the people who are counting them."

Father Teaches Priesthood Duty to Son

By Jack B. Kimball

SANTA CLARITA, CA—The Saturday after Curt Whitehead's twelve-year-old son, Steve, received the Aaronic Priesthood, his father took him out to the garage to teach him one of the most important priesthood duties.

"First I showed him how to prime the lawn mower engine, and then we started it up," Whitehead said. "Before we took it out on the lawn, we said a little prayer for safety and guidance. Then I showed him how to mow diagonally in one direction, then mow it again in the opposite direction, just the way the Lord likes it."

Wiping the sweat from his forehead, Steve said, "Dad taught me that no other success can compensate for failure to keep our lawn perfect. Too bad my older sister can't help, but that would be like asking her to pass the sacrament."

Youth Give Best Leader Awards

By Kylee-Ashlee Cannon Christiansen

OGDEN, UTAH—In a stirring show of youthful enthusiasm and solidarity, the young men and young women of the Ogden 23rd Ward put on a Best Leader Awards night last Wednesday to honor their Young Men, Young Women, Scouting, and Sunday school leaders.

"It's like our leaders never get any recognition for the cool stuff they do, like dyeing their hair purple or letting us do doughnuts in their Camaros in the church parking lot after dark," noted Carson Pierce, age seventeen. "So we all kinda got together and thought we'd give our coolest leaders some awards and stuff."

Among those honored was youth Sunday school teacher Mindy McTavish. "Mindy is so awesome because she never makes us call her Sister McTavish, like our bratty Young Women president keeps telling us to do," says twelve-year-old Chloe Ann Patterson. "Also, she let us have a sleepover at her house and gave us all these sex quizzes from *Seventeen* to answer. I mean, like, how cool is that? She told us not to tell our moms, and I was like, duh, like we would." ▶

Another Beehive, Anna Lundquist, adds, "Plus, she totally always ends Sunday lessons fifteen minutes early and talks with us about the boys we like and how we should kiss them and stuff. And she has a Ouija Board!"

"He never plans gay things like yard work for widows or singing at the old folks' home."

The Young Men recognized their president, Travis Quimby, "because he never makes us do service like our old president did," says Brad Manning, age fourteen. "He thinks service is a good idea, but it's too hard. He laughed and said he was too lazy. I was all, right on." Manning's classmate Kyle Warner agrees with the assessment: "Travis is so rad. He never plans gay things like yard work for widows or singing at the old folks' home. We play basketball for our meetings, or sometimes we even hang at his house and play Nintendo. Like, once we all played Resident Evil for, like, eight hours straight. It ripped, dude."

The group was unanimous in awarding highest honors to Denise Eider, the Young Women first counselor, "just for being so completely awesome," says Mia Maid Kate Meyers. "The best lesson we ever had was when Denise went off on how she'd gotten pregnant when she was fourteen. She talked about how sad it was and stuff, but what was awesome was when she told us what she did to snag the high school quarterback! When she was only fourteen! That was a good lesson. I won't forget it anytime soon."

Although the young men have heard Eider's lessons only on a few fifth Sundays when the Young Men and Young Women combined, they agreed she should get top honors. "Dude, she flirts with me, she's divorced, and she's totally hot," says Derek

Killian, age seventeen. "Plus, she once caught me smoking, but she told me it was no big deal. As long as I didn't do it enough to get addicted, I wouldn't have to see the bishop. She's totally the best youth leader we've ever had."

Bishop Thomas M. Ricks was unable to attend the awards ceremony, which was held in Kate Meyers's basement, but he says that he supports his youth leaders. "Our Young Men and Young Women presidencies really do have a remarkable rapport with our youth, as I have seen many times," he says. "They have all bonded well and have so much in common."

The parents are proud of the youth leaders' achievements. "I don't know what they're doing in their Wednesday night activities, but whatever it is, I hope they keep it up," says Marnie Lundquist, Anna's mother. "That Denise Eider is single-handedly responsible for my daughter's renewed interest in church, which she never attended when Lori [Hunter] was Young Women president. It's just nice to know that people like them are taking an interest in our kids' futures."

DON'T BOTHER ME. I'M **FASTING**.

Girls' Camp Teaches Free Agency

By Kylee-Ashlee Cannon Christiansen

WEBER COUNTY, UT—Young Women leaders of the Brighton South Stake are calling this year's camp "a real big hit." Planned around the theme "Free to Choose," this year's camp is teaching the girls memorable lessons about the value of free agency.

The emphasis on free agency started at the first planning meeting, according to camp director Maren Johansen. "We planned the whole camp using the girls' ideas," she said. "We listened to each idea and used every one that we could." For example, the girls wanted tacos, salad, and strawberry ice cream for their big dinner on Friday night. "We leaders hate tacos, and the girls don't need any ice cream, really—the sugar makes them hyper, but we are having the salad," said Johansen.

The leaders even let the girls have freedom of choice when packing their camp supplies. "We let them bring eye shadow this time, because this camp is about choice," says Johansen's assistant Rhoda Hancock. "As long as the eye shadow is really pale pink, that is. And as long as they don't over-apply it. I had to confiscate some berry-colored shadow, unfortunately."

"To qualify for breakfast, the girls have to say something about free agency in their testimonies."

The stake's long-standing proscriptions remain in effect against shorts, cap-sleeved and sleeveless shirts, sandals, clothes with logos or slogans (except for the stake camp slogan for the current year only), earrings of any kind, and "gaudy ponytail holders." According to Hancock, "These rules are for the girls' safety and so no one gets offended. Those things distract from a learning environment, and we really want them to learn about free agency."

Turning to a young woman, Hancock said, "No, Lacey, don't use the blue paint on that. No, the red, not the blue. No, use the red. The blue will look really stupid. No, look at this one I did. See? You need the red." Hancock then excused herself to round up all the girls, make them put away their crafts, and walk them over to the assembly spot, where they would sit and learn about personal freedom for three inspiring hours.

To encourage participation during the culminating testimony meeting, the leaders are planning to use their "inspiring motivational idea" from last year: no breakfast on Saturday morning for those who don't bear their testimonies. "What a great and positive motivator that will be!" says Johansen. "To qualify for breakfast, the girls have to say something about free agency in their testimonies."

The girls all echo the leaders' enthusiasm about this year's camp. "I'm learning that free agency is a good thing to have, because my leaders keep telling me it is," said Shannon Taylor, a Beehive. Melinda Walker, a Laurel, added, "If I go to camp all six years, Mom's going to get me a scooter. So I guess it's worth it."

Righteous Youth Destroy Evil Music

By Teancum Zenos Smoot IV

PROVO, UT—Following the exhortations of a recent Education Week lecture, Ferris Yount and his LDS friends have decided to smash their inappropriate CDs, including those with profane and obscene lyrics and those recorded by artists who don't keep the standards of the gospel.

"It was a tough decision," admits Yount, who has a large music collection, "but the spirit was so strong at Education Week that I just knew it was the right thing to do."

Inspired by the story he heard about righteous youth taking a sledgehammer to CDs, Yount and his friends held a special fireside outside the Helaman Halls dormitory on BYU campus. After an opening prayer, Robert Bailey gave a two-and-a-half minute talk on the influence of music. Then the smashing began.

"It felt great, just fantastic," said Jerry Trimble, still sweating from his turn at the hammer. "As I obliterated those suckers, I swear I could see evil spirits rising from them. I knew right then we were doing the work of the Lord."

"Crud like that can worm its way into your mind subliminally."

The first CD to go was Carl Orff's symphonic chorale *Carmina Burana*.

"I can't even believe I listened to that crap," said Trimble. "I mean, it's all a bunch of stuff about monks having sex and drinking. It's all in Latin, but crud like that can worm its way into your mind subliminally."

Also found among the wreckage were Richard Wagner's *Seigfried*, a three-hour opera that includes an incident of incest in its story; Puccini's *Madama Butterfly* for its final suicide scene; and J.S. Bach's *Goldberg Variations*, which Bailey described as "music written for the bedroom, if you know what I mean."

Many of Handel's works felt the brunt of the young men's righteousness. Apparently the lyrics of the old Austrian's music take the name of God in vain "too many times to count," according to Yount.

Not stopping at overtly evil music, the group smashed CDs by artists of questionable moral integrity.

"You know Mozart was a real womanizer?" gasped Yount as he demolished W.A. Mozart's *Air on a G-String*. "Besides that, G-string? Come on, Amadeus! Get your mind out of the gutter."

The work of many so-called Impressionists, including Maurice Ravel and Claude Debussy, met similar fates. "Just look at the way they dressed," said Trimble. "Definitely flamers. And they drank like fish! I'm not having that stuff ruining the spirit of my apartment."

Spirituality Testing Starts in Pilot Stakes

By Kylee-Ashlee Cannon Christiansen

AUBURN, TX—Due to "a lack of data regarding the effectiveness of youth training," the Church Educational System this week finished a yearlong project of administering a new series of gospel aptitude tests for children and youth. CES spokesman Jason Pinegar said, "These tests will help us track and target future church leaders as well as identify and isolate kids who will have huge testimony issues farther down the road."

The tests, called Testimony Health Indicators, are given to children every year from age three to eighteen. The extensive, in-depth questions are designed to "encourage self-awareness and cultivate increased spirituality," according to Pinegar. "They also reveal vital information about these kids, including innermost thoughts, an area that was previously closed to church scrutiny."

For instance, eight-year-old Abbie Fielding's recent test asked, "Do your mommy and daddy pray together every day on their knees? If so, how happy does that make you feel? If not, in how many possible ways could they be damaging your spiritual growth?"

> **"The purpose is not to intimidate the child. Rather, it's to go through his or her psyche in great detail to ensure absolute conformity to LDS practices and beliefs."**

Her fourteen-year-old brother, Alex, answered questions such as, "How many times a week do you have inappropriate thoughts about the opposite sex? Describe one of them here in detail" and "What have you done lately that you don't want to confess? Why?"

The three-hour tests are administered at the end of May by an official proctor, after an intensive four-week study and review period. The tests are then sent to Salt Lake City, where a recently formed committee, the Spiritual Growth Advisory (SGA) Board, analyzes each test according to a complicated set of standards called Spiritual Growth Enhancement Predictors.

"We do much more than just grade true/false, multiple-choice tests," says an anonymous committee member. "We apply an advanced series of algorithms to these youngsters' writings, analyzing handwriting, hand/pen movements, and even folds in the page. All of these reveal much about the developing spirituality of these kids and can help us head off the problems with church authority that so often rear their ugly heads during the teenage years."

He added, "The tests also help our youth be more like Jesus."

When a test reveals that an LDS child or youth is having trouble, the leaders go out of their way to help. Four local leaders and four SGA members invite the child or teen to meet with them for a four-hour video-recorded chat session, held in the bishop's office. "The purpose is not to intimidate the child," said an SGA member. "Rather, it is to go through his or her psyche in great detail and convince the subject that absolute conformity to church practices and beliefs is optimal for his or her ecclesiastical future." He added that ▶

the answers help SGA members identify other members, such as parents or teachers, who may need "spiritual counseling."

Stake president Darryl Heissen calls the tests "a highly effective tool" to help him meet the spiritual needs of his members. For example, the initial round of tests revealed that a young woman, age thirteen, was having trouble with self-image. "Through extensive additional questioning, she finally divulged that her father was seen in the company of a single woman at the last ward party," Heissen explained. "We called him in for questioning and ended up taking away his temple recommend. And his wife's as well, for reasons too complicated to go into here."

President Heissen added, "These tests really help me to love my members and administer to them in a Christ-like way."

Currently the tests are being given only in five pilot stakes around the country, but if they prove useful, the CES will expand the program nationwide next year.

Chapter 2:
In the Trenches with God's Army

Two by two, Mormon missionaries march across nearly this entire planet, knocking on doors and sharing the gospel. In fact, with their immediately recognizable uniforms, militaristic organization into districts and zones, and rallying causes of fighting against the adversary and winning souls to the kingdom, this worldwide missionary force is often described as "God's army."

Always keen to provide compelling wartime reportage, *The Mormon Tabernacle Enquirer* imbeds courageous reporters among the missionaries in hotspots the world over. From an innovative new use for the methane gas produced in the Missionary Training Center to groundbreaking missionary efforts in Japan, Ethiopia, and the Philippines, the *Enquirer* brings you a missionary perspective that you simply can't get anywhere else, not even from the *Church News*.

MTC Now Powered by Its Own Methane

By M. Spencer Pratt

PROVO, UT—Officials today confirmed that because of a successful alternative energy experiment, the Missionary Training Center in Provo is now powered entirely with methane produced by the hundreds of missionaries living there.

"The MTC's food has long been notorious for causing these, uh, emissions," said spokesman Carl Spainhower. "We wondered if we could harness them for some good use. The church has always encouraged thriftiness and self-sufficiency."

Methane produced by the missionaries rises to the ceilings of their classrooms and dormitories, where it is collected by air intakes. A complex system of pumps, filters, and pipelines separates the methane from the rest of the air and sends it to a newly installed power plant, where it is converted into electricity.

Workers among the complex array of baffles, manifolds, and pipelines that will carry the freshly minted methane to the processing furnaces in the basement. "It's tricky work," says Johnny Nguyen, a subcontractor for the job. "The last thing anyone wants is a leak."

"If we were to double the frequency of pizza day, we could also power at least three nearby BYU buildings."

"We're very excited by our results so far," said Spainhower. "Not only are we producing all the electricity we need, but our numbers indicate that if we were to double the frequency of pizza day, we could also power at least three nearby BYU buildings. We're also looking closely at BYU dormitories as an additional source of power."

Reactions among MTC missionaries were varied. "I think it's—oh, excuse me—great," said Elder Jeb King, from Layton, Utah. "We're here to serve however—oops, sorry—we can. My companion and I have been—whew!—competing to see who can generate more kilowatt hours."

Sister Ashley Nelson, on the other hand, said the project is "so disgusting, I don't even want to think about it. Only a man could come up with something like this."

Missionary Now Curses with Near-Native Proficiency

By Kylee-Ashlee Cannon Christiansen

KYOTO, JAPAN—Elder Spencer Norris of Highland, Utah, knows that hard work and study can really pay off for a missionary. Having arrived in the Japan Kobe Mission a mere eight months ago, he recently stunned his district by winning the area-wide Missionary Curse-Off.

"Besides studying the regular dictionary words, you really have to get out and understand the culture," said Elder Norris when asked about his winning secret. "For instance, you can learn mild words like *aho* [idiot] and stuff from a dictionary, but to learn how to say phrases like *Anta wa yagiseppite iru kijo no kiji desu* [you are a goat-kissing abandoned child of a she-devil] you really have to get out and talk to the common man. And that's the most rewarding part of the whole thing."

Elder Norris claims that these strategies led to his winning phrase: "*Anta no zousaku kara haha wa byouki tsuchibuta to sakatta no o wakatte iru.*" [I gather from your facial features that your mother mated with a diseased aardvark.]

Extra points are given for appropriate gestures and facial grimaces.

Elder Norris cited careful study of the missionary discussions as a key to his success. "Oh, yeah, you can learn great words like *makai* [hell] and *kokuhyou* [damnation] from the discussions. You have to study the *hanashis* [discussions] with due diligence, or else you really haven't done your homework."

When asked for advice for other missionaries seeking to win the contest, Elder Norris said, "'Seek not to declare my word, but first seek to obtain my word, and then shall your tongue be loosed,' That's the D&C, chapter 11, verse 21."

Despite the accolades and admiration of his fellow missionaries, Elder Norris remains low key. For example, he has not told his mission president about his accomplishment. "I'm just out to do this for myself and for the people of Japan. If I, or you, or anyone, told the *booch* [mission president], then I'd already have my earthly reward. I'd rather lay it up in heaven." He added, "Besides, I'm not sure that [President Clarke] would really understand."

The origins of the Kobe mission's twice-yearly Missionary Curse-Off are unknown, although it remains one of the most popular activities in the mission. Extra points are given for appropriate gestures and facial grimaces.

Missionary Accidentally Calls Prophet "Dude"

KIEV, UKRAINE—Elder Edward Appleby, a Utah native serving in the Ukraine Kiev Mission, was embarrassed when he inadvertently addressed President Gordon B. Hinckley as "dude" when meeting him at a church gathering in Ukraine's capitol city.

"I have no idea why I said it," said Appleby. "It was a total mistake."

Elder Wes Sterling, Appleby's current missionary companion and trainer, recounted the incident. "We were waiting in line with a bunch of other guys from our area waiting to shake the prophet's hand. We'd just had this really spiritual meeting, and everyone was really quiet—no one was goofing around or anything. When it was Appleby's turn to shake President Hinckley's hand, he said, 'What's up, dude?' and gave the prophet this really aggressive handshake. I was freakin' horrified."

Appleby, visibly shaken after his unorthodox—albeit unintended—greeting, said nothing further. President Hinckley reportedly gave Appleby a benign response and quietly continued on to the next missionary in line.

"I guess it just slipped out," explained Appleby. "I hope my mom doesn't find out about this. She's real churchy—she teaches Gospel Doctrine and everything. Something like this would really piss her off—uh, I mean disappoint her."

"He's always doing stupid stuff, like trying to cut his own hair, but this one takes the freakin' cake."

In Sterling's opinion, "Appleby will never live this one down. He's always doing stupid stuff, like trying to cut his own hair, but this one takes the freakin' cake." Shaking his head, Sterling concluded, "Freak, I still can't believe he called the prophet 'dude.' Freakin' greenie."

President Hinckley could not be reached for comment.

North American Missionary Work Goes Online

SALT LAKE CITY—At a news conference, officials announced a major change in the way the church will conduct missionary work. Because of explosive growth in third-world countries, the number of full-time missionaries there will be doubled, with a corresponding decrease in North America.

To fill the gap caused by the reassignment of thousands of missionaries, the church has developed VirtualElder.org, where the missionary discussions will be taught online.

According to spokesman Tom Tolbert, online discussions will have several advantages. "A discussion can now be taught at any time, day or night," he said. "Imagine you are watching a late-night rerun of *Family Guy* and you see an LDS commercial that piques your curiosity. Instead of calling the 800 number and waiting days for the missionaries, now you can log onto the Internet and receive the first discussion right away."

According to Tolbert, VirtualElder.org will be completely interactive. "Viewers can have the discussions taught by an onscreen elder of their own race, in six languages or four English dialects: Deep South, Brooklyn, Western Drawl, and Gangsta," he explained.

Assembled members of the media watched a PowerPoint presentation that demonstrated how live elders would be replaced by virtual missionaries. Following a video clip of a prophet preaching the gospel, an onscreen elder asks, "How does it make you feel to know that prophets are still receiving revelation today?" A dropdown menu then appears, and the viewer is asked to select the answer that best reflects his or her feelings at the time. Among the choices are such responses as "I have a burning in my bosom," "That's really cool," "They never taught us about this in Vacation Bible School," and, in the case of the Gangsta version, "Even mo' betta!"

The website is so interactive, continued Tolbert, that if the viewer chooses an appropriate response to a question about how they feel, the virtual elder will confirm that what they are feeling is inspiration.

A pair of virtual elders will appear in a popup box and ask if the viewer would like to hear a special message.

When the prospective convert answers a predetermined number of questions correctly, a baptismal challenge will be issued. If the challenge is accepted, dropdown menus will appear and the investigator will be able to schedule the date, time, and location of his or her baptism. Each mission home in North America will receive the Baptismal Service Requests (BSRs) for their area, and the mission president will assign missionaries to fill the font and conduct the service.

Website upgrades are already in the works. Soon the virtual elders will perform service just as the live elders do, carrying out such tasks as automatically installing BYUNet as the investigator's Internet browser or purging pornography files from the hard drive.

Virtual tracting is scheduled to begin ▶

by the end of the year, complete with door-knock sound effects and a pair of elders appearing in a popup box asking if you would like to hear a special message.

"It used to take a hundred or more missionaries to cover the typical mission," declared

Supreme Court Ruling Disappoints Missionaries
By Jack B. Kimball

SALT LAKE CITY—Missionaries throughout the United States reacted with disappointment to the Supreme Court ruling favoring the Jehovah Witnesses over an Ohio town that wanted to curtail door-to-door soliciting.

"In effect, the Supreme Court has condemned me to thousands of hours of more door-knocking," said Elder Jason Robinson, a missionary in Louisville, Kentucky, with eight months left on his mission. "We were really hoping the tide would turn and we could stop bugging people at their doors. Anything would be better than tracting."

"Dude, I am so disappointed," said Elder Carl Everson of the Colorado Denver Mission. "Hardly anyone is ever home when we tract, except old farts, unemployed people, and housewives who might try to seduce us. I'll tell you what, if missionaries or any kind of salesman knocked on my door, I wouldn't be happy about it. Sometimes I feel like a hypocrite out here. We're lower on the food chain than telemarketers."

"I'm jealous of my friend in Thailand," said Elder Ryan Hatch of the Massachusetts Boston Mission. "Tracting is illegal there, so all they do is set up street displays and visit members. Yeah, freedom of speech is important, but I think it's wrong to intrude on people's private property. Isn't there something in the Constitution about that?"

However, not all missionaries are disappointed. "I love tracting," said Elder Preston

Tolbert. "Now it can be done with just a handful. It's our obligation to make full use of this great computer tool."

Richards, a zone leader and aspiring assistant to the president in the Montana Billings Mission. "It really gives me a feeling of building the kingdom. It doesn't matter how effective tracting is—what matters is that I'm anxiously engaged in a good cause. I like to think each door erases another one of my sins."

"I just hope it's true that the more doors you knock, the sexier your future wife gets."

Missionary department manager James Anderson concurs. "Tracting helps turn these young brethren into willing vessels of righteousness. It humbles them. I'm frankly glad it isn't easy, because this generation already has it too easy in so many ways. We never said it would be easy, we just said it would be worth it. And make no mistake, tracting is worth it on the eternal scale."

Two weeks away from his release, President Lincoln Boyce of the California Sacramento Mission disagrees with tracting. "The converts who stay active are the ones brought in by friends or family members. The handful of people we find tracting just don't make good converts. And it takes the boys so long to find them."

"Yeah, this was a setback," said Elder Hatch, bending over to clip his pant leg so it wouldn't catch in his bicycle chain. "I just hope it's true that the more you tract, the sexier your future wife gets."

Missionary Couple Cheered by "Plucky" Ethiopian Branch's Fasting

By M. Spencer Pratt

MOSCOW, ID—According to recently returned missionary couple Robert and Edna Simpson, the branch in Addis Ababa, Ethiopia, has set a record for fasting, with over ninety percent of the members having fasted every Sunday for five or more years.

"Those wonderful Saints were such an inspirational example to me," said Brother Simpson, who served as the branch president. "It was so touching to see them go without food week after week, exercising their faith on behalf of those who had even less than they did. Of course, most of them didn't seem to fully understand the concept. Fast offerings were surprisingly low, considering how much fasting was going on. I used to speak on that subject week after week, trying to get them to understand that fasting without contributing is just starving, but I never did seem to get through."

"At first, most of the people we taught tried to boil their Books of Mormon into soup instead of reading them."

"They really were such sweet spirits," added Sister Simpson. "It was so inspiring to go to a place where the church is so new. Why, at first most of the people we taught tried to boil their Books of Mormon into soup instead of reading them. But word finally got around that we were there to teach them, not feed them. That's when we were really able to figure out who the elect were. They needed our help so badly."

"Yes, there were a lot of misconceptions we had to deal with," said Brother Simpson. "Why, I remember the problems we used to have at sacrament meeting. We eventually had to start serving the sacrament only once a month, because some people's kids were totally out of control, grabbing all the bread they could get and stuffing it all in their mouths. That turned out to be a blessing in disguise, because we'd get a lot of nonmembers to church on the weeks when we did serve the sacrament. But then our deacon started making off with the leftovers."

When the *Enquirer* contacted Umbwe Yasima, a member of the Simpsons' branch, to confirm the impressive fasting record, he commented, "Please, need food. Oh, blessed food."

"Missionary Position" Allegedly Inappropriate

OGDEN, UT—Sister Stella Reeves of the Ogden 44th Ward is circulating a petition asking for church leaders to rename the missionary position.

"Everyone knows missionaries shouldn't even be having sex, so the very name promotes sin," says Reeves. "Missionaries don't need any excuse to fool around."

Reeves suggests that the church change the name to "the bishop position, the celestial position, or the one right and true position for husbands and wives eternally married and wanting to conceive children."

Area Man's Mission Years Really Were His Best
By M. Spencer Pratt

OGDEN, UT—"It's been all downhill since then," said local plumbing supply salesman Jim Barton, age forty-seven, about the two years he spent on his LDS mission, which ended twenty-six years ago. In retrospect, Barton confirms that his mission was, in fact, the best years of his life.

"A lot of people come home from their missions and say they were the best years of their lives," Barton said. "What do they have to compare them to? High school? Big contest there. But compared to nearly half a friggin' century of life experience, I've realized that those twenty-four months in Brazil really were the best time of my life. I dropped out of college after two years and married Kathy, and I've been working at her dad's place ever since. That pretty much sums it up."

Staring gloomily into the distance, Barton continued: "I mean, back then, I used to bring people the most important message there could possibly be, changing their lives immeasurably for the good. Now I bring people reasonably priced U-bends. Not exactly comparable, is it?"

Not even Barton's experiences in the church have lived up to his expectations. "Back on the mish, I thought that by the time I was this age, I'd be a bishop or stake president or maybe even a GA. Instead, I find myself teaching Sunday school to the high school freshmen. Jeez. Back when I was an AP, I was in charge of the physical and spiritual well-being of over a hundred missionaries. Now I'm in charge of a half-dozen teenagers for an hour a week."

Barton added, "Oh, yeah, I swear occasionally now too. I never used to do that back then. Crap. What's happened to my life?"

When asked if his wife and children, Jesse (age seventeen) and Charles (fifteen), have given his life some meaning, Barton replied, "Yeah, OK, the family life has had its moments—my wedding day, the days my kids were born—but generally we just tolerate each other. It's usually more hassle than anything else. It's nothing like the relationship I had with this one companion of mine. He was great." Barton then quickly added, "Wait, it wasn't like that."

> **"I used to bring people the most important message there could possibly be. Now I bring people reasonably priced U-bends."**

Barton has toyed with plans to regain his former glory. "I guess I could look forward to retiring and going on another mission with Kathy. But when I tried bringing it up the other day, she didn't seem too interested. She said something about how she'd be able to scrapbook all day when we're retired. Not one word about doing church work. In fact, I think she thinks scrapbooking *is* church work. Oh, well. Maybe it will all work out in the next life."

SpongeBob Receives Mission Call

By Milton P. Romney

BIKINI BOTTOM—Local celebrity and Krabby-patty chef SpongeBob SquarePants announced at this week's sacrament services of the Bikini Bottom Branch that he has received a call to serve in the Japan Tokyo North Mission. Elder SquarePants reports to the MTC in September.

News of the mission call came as a surprise to some, many of whom were not even aware that SquarePants is a Mormon. "He's such a wholesome, hard-working, dedicated little invertebrate, I should have known," said Sandy Squirrel, a Baptist. "Even though he's yellow and absorbent, he isn't pushy or self-righteous or anything. He's porous—he'll make a fine missionary."

Not everyone has been supportive of Elder SquarePants's desire to serve a mission, most notably Elder Boyd K. Plankton.

Mr. Krabbs, proprietor of the Krusty Krabb and employer of Elder SquarePants for most of his career, says he'll miss his best patty cook. "'Tis my hope the little lad doesn't end up in a sushi roll somewhere in Tokyo. I'll be keeping his spatula at the ready for his return."

Not everyone has been supportive of Elder SquarePants's desire to serve a mission, most notably Elder Boyd K. Plankton, who initially accused SpongeBob of having unnatural affections for his best friend and neighbor, Patrick Starfish. During a fireside, Elder Plankton criticized the pineapple-inhabiting sponge of being "strangely effeminate" and "living with a fellow invertebrate by the name of Gary," both of which he claimed were clear indicators of his sexual orientation. "Anyone can tell that SpongeBob SquarePants, who

regularly cavorts about in his square underpants, is a flaming homosexual," a charge that Elder SquarePants denied.

"You'll never get the secret of my sexuality from me, Elder Plankton!" SquarePants said on the Dave Letterman show the following month.

Since that time, Elder Plankton has reversed his position, which ultimately cleared the path for SquarePants to receive his mission call. "I've seen the SpongeBob movie," admitted Elder Plankton. "It's a great film, with a wholesome good-conquers-evil theme, much the same as the Book of Mormon. And I didn't realize that Gary was his pet. I jumped to an unfortunate conclusion."

Elder Plankton reluctantly stated that SpongeBob's developmentally delayed neighbor Patrick, on the other hand, could never serve a mission, as he will never grow a foot or two. "He's a starfish. He can grow only arms," Plankton said. "Besides, it still bothers me that he did that final scene in the movie wearing stiletto heels and fishnet stockings. The boy's not right."

The Bikini Bottom Branch has scheduled Elder SquarePants's farewell for August 26, after which a party has been scheduled at the Easter Island Statue of Squidward, who is thrilled to see his annoying neighbor leave for two years.

Missionaries Crush Baptismal Record

By Milton P. Romney

MANILA, PHILIPPINES—Elders Frank Jachumson and Carl Ritter of the Philippines Manila Mission recently broke the church-wide record for same-day baptisms.

According to Jachumson, the two companions were returning to the island of Bohol from a zone conference on Cebu when their ferry ran aground close to shore. After the elders dove into the sea along with the other passengers, the quick-thinking companions muttered the baptismal prayer while treading water.

"Today we welcomed 649 new members," said a smiling Elder Ritter.

Corrections

We mistakenly reported that a mission president in Chile had castrated some missionaries for not making the most of their companionship study time. That sentence should have read "castigated," not "castrated." We received a great deal of mail from concerned parents, and we regret any alarm or inconvenience we might have caused.

In our recent article on financial preparedness, we inadvertently stated that the prophet is going to start predicting winning Powerball numbers in the *Church News*. That information will continue to be made available only to the church's financial department, where it is used for wisely investing tithing revenues. The *Enquirer* regrets any disappointment our readers may suffer as a result of this error.

Contrary to what we reported in our last issue, increasing your intake of salsa does not improve spirituality. However, it does give you a burning sensation.

Views from the Street

The church no longer allows missionary farewells and open houses. What's your opinion about that?

"No farewell party? Heck, now where's my motivation for going?"

"No problem. Our stake can send out the high councilmen more often. Everyone loves those Sundays."

"Wow, prayers really do get answered! I was dreading singing that song my mom made all my brothers sing."

"Blast. I was planning on replacing the sacrament bread with mini-taquitos when my son left for Guatemala."

"We're holding our open house in the basement, and you have to know the code word to get in."

"I guess I can wait till fast Sunday to tell that funny story about eight-year-old Danny, his dirty underpants, and that busload of Catholic girls."

Chapter 3:
All I Really Need to Know I Learned at BYU

N estled in the heart of the most conservative county of the most conservative U.S. state, Brigham Young University is a beardless, bellybuttonless, caffeine-free bastion of academic nonfreedom. Historically, one of the university's slogans was "Enter to learn, go forth to serve," but that has recently been updated to "Enter to conform, go forth to earn." Another main slogan, "The world is our campus," was recently amended as follows: "The world is our campus—however, we are definitely not worldly." (The size of the sign had to be doubled to fit that one.)

BYU exerts such a powerful influence throughout Mormondom that the *Enquirer* keeps half a dozen undercover reporters on campus at all times—unfortunately, we must continually replace our single female reporters, because they keep getting married and becoming full-time homemakers. We were the first to break the story on Starbucks building a special café on campus, the new "beer cards" allowing consumption of beer for medical reasons, the launch of the scrapbooking degree program, and many other groundbreaking developments.

BYU Offers Scrapbooking Degree

By Kylee-Ashlee Cannon Christiansen

PROVO, UT—Brigham Young University's College of Humanities announced that it is now offering a four-year bachelor's degree in the scrapbooking arts. Humanities Dean Loren W. Huish calls the new degree "an idea whose time has come" and "a real boon to the many LDS women who are looking for a way to legitimize their talent."

The university has hired nine full-time professors and an administrator to oversee the scrapbooking degree program. Each new faculty member holds an advanced certificate from Creative Photobooks, a company that runs grueling five-day scrapbook workshops all over the country. Called Creative Photobooks University, or CPU, the program has awarded masters and doctorates of scrapology (M.Scrap and D.Scrap, respectively) to thousands of women in the last two years.

"We actively recruited CPU graduates who demonstrated superior cropping abilities," explained Huish. All of BYU's scrapbooking arts professors have extensive publication credentials, with at least five completed scrapbooks on their CVs. "Five," emphasized Huish. "They've all created at least five entire scrapbooks. That's a lot."

The degree requires a minimum of 45 credit hours of scrapbooking arts classes, on top of the usual general education and elective requirements. Students must take Scrapbooking Basics 1 and 2, Design and Layout Basics, and History of Scrapbooking. After those required classes, they can fill the rest of their hours from electives such as the following:

- Sticker Enhancements: Can They Be *Too* Cute?
- From Beary to Somebunny: A Scrapper's Essential Vocabulary
- "It's Genealogy, Honey": Legitimizing Sabbath Scrapbooking
- 8 1/2 x 11 Paper or 12 x 12? The Controversy Rages On

The response to the new degree has been overwhelming, and the professors are already teaching to overfull classrooms. Discussions are ongoing about possibly creating two program emphases—scrapbook and memory book—to address the students' differing interests. "Memory books are totally different from scrapbooks," says instructor Terri Pulliam, M.Scrap. "They focus on telling someone's life story with photographs to illustrate, while scrapbooks focus on telling someone's life story through photographs." However, the creation of emphases will most likely wait a year or two until the program has stabilized.

> **"This new degree gives girls something college-ish to do until they find their husbands."**

BYU students are thrilled with the new degree. "This is, like, soooo cool," says BYU freshman Colette Neubaum, who claimed that she had "totally no idea" what to major in before the degree was announced. "I took a few classes in psychology with my friend, but they are way hard! I mean, you have to read books and everything, and I was developing these awful little wrinkly lines. Hello, like I need the stress. But now I can do my scrapbooks and get a college degree at the same time!"

Unexpectedly, the scrapbooking arts degree has won fans further afield—in BYU's College of Family Sciences, for instance. "We just had too many students who wanted a family, marriage, and child degree rather than anything rigorous or with earning potential," said instructor Tammy Hayes. "I'm glad this new scrapbooking degree came along to give these girls something collegeish to do until they find their husbands."

BYU president Cedric Matheson expressed pleasure as he endorsed the new degree. "This new program will help strengthen LDS families in many ways," he predicted. "I exhort our female scrapbooking graduates to take their skills into their homes, leave the paying careers to the menfolk, and use their talents to bless their families and fill their bookshelves."

BYU Student Uses Commitment Pattern to Get Date

By LeVoy Mann

PROVO, UT—Twenty-two-year-old Patrick Foley recently used the missionary commitment pattern when he approached fellow BYU student Linda Sampson for a date. During his mission to Argentina, Foley mastered this pattern to baptize thirty-six people. "I want to baptize this chick in my love," he says.

Foley's first step was to prepare Sampson by cracking jokes and complimenting her dress as they walked home from church. "On my mission, we had to prepare people by helping them feel the spirit," Foley said. "In this case, I just had to warm her up with some humor and flattery."

Next, Foley issued a clear, direct invitation to Sampson: "Will you attend the basketball game with me on Saturday night?" When she politely declined, he moved into the third stage of the commitment pattern: following up. He learned that she did not care for basketball and was more interested in attending a movie with her roommates that night.

To overcome these obstacles, Foley employed the fourth and final step in the commitment pattern: resolving concerns. "I have to admit, Lisa's concerns were a lot easier to resolve than people on my mission," he said. "It was really hard to talk people into paying tithing, quitting coffee, and ignoring our polygamous history." Foley offered to take Sampson to the restaurant and movie of her choice, and he suggested that one of her roommates might like to double with them.

"I have to admit, Lisa's concerns were a lot easier to resolve than people on my mission."

When Sampson finally agreed, Foley ended the conversation by bearing his testimony about his confidence in their mutual enjoyment of the date. "If everything goes well, maybe I'll use the commitment pattern to get her to marry me."

Starbucks to Open at BYU
By Lisa Layton

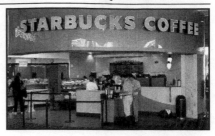

PROVO, UT—Starbucks Coffee is found almost everywhere: in strip malls, in Barnes and Noble bookstores, in airports, and on college campuses. But one place you won't find them is on the Provo, Utah, campus of Brigham Young University, which is owned by the church, whose dietary codes prohibit the consumption of coffee and tea.

Until now, that is. No, it's not that the church has changed its codes. Representatives for Starbucks have announced that a new café to be built in the BYU Student Center will not sell coffee, not even decaf. Instead, it will sell only hot chocolate, certain soft drinks, and bakery items.

"The Mormon market was one of the last we had left to break into," said Mark G. Bean of Starbucks. "We found that many Mormons were hesitant to buy anything from Starbucks, even hot chocolate or a croissant. We couldn't even get them in the door. We didn't ever expect to sell coffee to them, but we thought that if we could show the Mormon college-age crowd that we sell items they like and can consume, we could increase our sales on non-coffee items by a significant margin."

"That really shows you how important the church has become."

Construction on the new café has already begun and should be completed within a few months. BYU issued a press release stating, "We are happy that a major retailer like Starbucks would adjust its products to suit our particular needs, and we are happy as well to offer our students an exceptionally delicious cup of hot chocolate."

BYU Student Association vice president Lance Stoker was initially jubilant when he heard of the arrangement. "That's so great, that a big chain like Starbucks would completely quit selling coffee so it could work with the church!" he exclaimed. "That really shows you how important the church has become."

However, upon learning that Starbucks would continue to sell coffee at its other locations, Stoker's enthusiasm became more cautious. He acknowledged that he was among those who had never entered a Starbucks and was uncertain as to whether or not he would patronize the new BYU café.

"I'll have to see what happens when it opens and find out from people who are a little more into experimentation than I am," he said. "I'm curious to find out whether this hot chocolate made with steamed milk and optional additional flavorings is really all that."

The agreement has generated controversy in other circles as well.

"At first I thought the decision was a little strange for the church," said Laverle Smith, president of the BYU Alumni Association. "I mean, Starbucks sells coffee, and we know we should avoid the very appearance of evil and not go into coffee shops, so why have one at BYU? But then I realized that the church and Starbucks are two of the fastest-growing organizations in the United States, if not the world. Between them, they will soon rule the planet. It makes sense that until the Second Coming, at least, the church should learn to coexist peacefully with Starbucks. Besides, they really do make the best hot chocolate."

BYU Reluctantly Starts Accepting "Beer Cards"

By Jack B. Kimball

PROVO, UT—Faced with mounting evidence that some individuals require regular beer consumption for optimal health, BYU has quietly started honoring doctor-signed "beer cards," similar to the "beard cards" long required for medically necessary facial hair.

"My patient gets terrible kidney stones if he doesn't keep beer flowing through his system," says Orem physician Lois P. Tucker. "Coke doesn't work." Provo doctor James O. McKay has a female patient who requires the yeasty compounds in beer to balance her intestinal flora.

Asked when psychiatrist-signed "queer cards" would start becoming accepted, a BYU spokesman refused to comment.

BYU Students Recommit to Wear Modest Clothing

By Teancum Zenos Smoot IV

PROVO, UT—The blessings of following the BYU dress code came to dramatic light only days after the "Goldifox and the Three Bares" poster showed up on campus last month. The poster, produced by the Student Honor Association, shows a "foxy" young woman whose "three bares" (the lower back, the midriff, and the chest) are covered.

Though some of the students ignored the poster, others courageously met its challenge. "I know that the Honor Association officers are inspired in what they do," said Gae Lynn Godfrey, a freshman majoring in biology. "So

I made sure I was covered. I gave all my questionable clothing to DI and bought a modest wardrobe from Eddie Bauer and the Gap. I made sure to get plenty so I wouldn't run out. I didn't want to chance being immodest."

Godfrey's example inspired many of her friends, who also bought slews of more modest clothing. "It was really a spiritual experience," said Cathy Crace, an art education major. "It was almost like the spirit was guiding me through the mall so I could find appropriate clothing."

> **"It was almost like the spirit was guiding me through the mall so I could find appropriate clothing."**

But the blessings didn't stop there. The girls who followed the admonition of the Goldifox poster have found that they cannot keep the campus men away. "I don't get it, but I'm not complaining," said Crace, showing off her calendar filled with dates.

Godfrey said she has been proposed to twice in the last week. "I think it was my obedience to the dress code that did it," she said. "Righteous young men are attracted to virtue."

Dan Clements, one of Godfrey's hopeful suitors, admits it was indeed the mysterious allure of Godfrey's clothing that attracted him. "I'm grateful that the young women have faith that we can look past their clothing and see, with our mind's eye, what really matters about a woman."

Hank Morton, a business major, said he would like to see a similar campaign targeted at men's modesty as well. "Sometimes you see these men who wear really tight pants and shirts that show their rippling muscles. That could really do things to people—especially girls. Because, you know, it doesn't bug me any."

BYU Chosen for Survivor Location

By LeVoy Mann

PROVO, UT—Get set for *Survivor: BYU.* CBS president and CEO Les Moonves announced that the next installment of the popular Survivor series will be shot at Brigham Young University for broadcast beginning in February. "BYU is very remote, but it's very scenic and provides a challenging backdrop for the series," says CBS spokesman Chris Ender. "We're very excited about this location."

Potential contestants had to agree to the school's stringent honor code and be interviewed by their local ecclesiastical leader prior to appearing on the show. Contestants will undergo physical challenges such as digging tunnels and rappelling down buildings. One of the challenges includes searching for a mythical eighty-year-old bottle of Grape Nehi soda pop somewhere in the lockers of the uncharted basement of the Harris Fine Arts Center.

Executive producer Mark Burnett says he wanted to take the show to a "completely different world that will astound and educate viewers. We spent months researching different locations around the world, weighing factors like culture, habitat, and local wildlife. The atmosphere of this school was like a whole new planet to us, and we hope viewers will agree."

Burnett added, "Past seasons have been all about physical hardship and challenge. But we wanted to try a different level and have people undergo some real extreme cultural challenges and privations. At BYU you can't drink, smoke, have sex, gamble, or even watch MTV. And these people—it's like a time warp to the 1950s!"

"The atmosphere of this school was like a whole new planet to us, and we hope viewers will agree."

Moonves, who is of the Jewish faith, says he wasn't wary about his show being immersed in a new religious culture. "This kind of thing is what the show's all about," he said. "That's why we put Richard Hatch and Rudy together [on the first *Survivor* series]. You have this military guy who outwardly doesn't like gays, and you put them on the same team. That's interesting theater. For *Survivor: BYU*, we've chosen contestants such as a pagan Wiccan girl, a single career woman from Manhattan, a black gang member from East Compton, and a member of Hell's Angels. Imagine the fun!"

Moonves spent two weeks on BYU's Provo campus. He says of the experience, "I couldn't wait to leave. If they weren't trying to convert me, they were trying to marry me off."

Know Your Mormon Terms

Home Leaching: When your home teachers keep showing up at dinnertime

Calling and Erection Made Sure: The promise of eternal increase in the hereafter

BYU-Idaho Students Relieved Austin Powers Movies Aren't R-Rated

By Terrill W. Cannon

REXBURG, ID—Last week members of a family home evening group at BYU-Idaho found themselves scurrying to double-check the rating of the video they were watching.

According to FHE group leader Cason Phillips of Orange County, California, the trouble started when a girl came down to practice piano in the lobby just when a particularly spicy scene was playing. She glanced at the television and said she thought she'd come to a school with standards.

"We were worried at first, but church standards really helped us out of a bind. We checked the video and found that the film was not R rated," Phillips said. When he told the offended party that the movie was only PG-13, she sat down and started watching.

According to Phillips, the girl was "laughing at Mini-Me and that thing Dr. Evil does with his little finger."

Lonnie Matheson, another member of the group, said, "That PG-13 rating for *The Spy Who Shagged Me*, like, really helped us choose the right. Plus, *Goldmember* looks hilarious. I don't think that one is R-rated either, which is good news for Mormons."

"I like knowing that the brethren think the Austin Powers movies are okay."

Regarding the FHE situation, Phillips is quick to point out that without the PG-13 rating, he and his friends might have had to shut down the activity, "which would have sucked," Phillips complained.

Likewise, Matheson pointed out that R-ratings can be really hard to figure out, be-cause "there are lots of movies like *Schindler's List, Braveheart,* and *Changing Lanes* that seem like good choices, but because they're R-rated, Satan has put all kinds of wicked things in there that would really hurt your testimony. I like knowing that the brethren think the Austin Powers movies are okay."

Phillips plans on serving a mission and doesn't want to stray onto dark paths. With a gleam in his eye, he says, "I hope I get called to England; that would be totally groovy, baby."

Snapshot

Most Common BYU Pickup Lines

You hang out at this temple often?

Mind if I peep in your seer stone?

Hey, what's your lineage?

Don't I know you from the preexistence?

That's a nice CTR tattoo.

What's a nice girl like you doing at a symposium like this?

Your bosom gives me a burning feeling.

BYU Professor Publicly Supports Michael Jackson

By David Patton Benson

PROVO, UT—In a statement released last Thursday, distinguished BYU professor Marsh Mathers, head of the prestigious Institute for Ethical Ethnicity Studies (IEES), announced that the various criminal charges of child molestation against pop star Michael Jackson have been, without exception, false. Mathers said his twenty-year study of Jackson's life and work provide "irrefutable evidence" that Jackson is "a just man, wrongfully accused."

In a recent interview, Mathers explained the reasons for his controversial stance. "It's actually very simple," Mathers said. "At the IEES, we have countless studies consistently showing a direct correlation between personal righteousness and skin tone. Michael Jackson's skin has been growing more white and delightsome over the passing years. I mean, everyone's noticed this. It's a staple of late-night comedy routines. But nobody has our body of evidence to suggest why his skin is growing lighter. It's obviously because of an increase in personal righteousness."

"Jackson's career, if looked at properly, shows his increasing commitment to righteous values."

Mathers said that Jackson's career, if looked at properly, shows his increasing commitment to righteous values. "Early in Michael's career, for example, you could see very inappropriate choreographic moves, including times when he would actually touch, you know, the front part of his trousers. He also moonwalked, sliding across the floor, which strongly suggests someone who has not anchored his life on a firmly righteous foundation. And look at his costume. One glove? Everyone knows what that signifies."

But Mathers points out that Jackson has changed. "He no longer gives public performances. It amazes me that no one else can see how significant that is. And he opened his Wonderland Ranch, so he could spend his days working with disadvantaged children and endangered animals. The soft glow of goodness you can see in his increasingly white, angelic face these days testifies to a life spent in the service of others."

Mathers believes that past criminal charges against Jackson have constituted religiously motivated persecution. "What you have is an entire legal system dedicated to calling good evil and evil good. It's a sure sign of the last days." He is relieved that Jackson was ultimately found not guilty. "Let's face it, Mormons aren't the only ones who believe a certain way. Lots of groups across the country have looked with an unbiased eye at clear evidence that correlates purity of heart with purity of skin. All Michael needed was the right jury, and he was home free."

Devil Possesses Apartment Complex Near BYU

By Jack B. Kimball

PROVO, UT—Within days after Brigham Young University withdrew approved housing status from Provo's Branbury Park apartment complex because "the environment is not conducive to moral and spiritual growth," signs of demonic possession began cropping up.

"I swear, I smell sulfur in the halls now, in addition to the tobacco smoke," said long-time tenant Lindsey Lund. "The other night, I heard a terrible voice chuckling at me from the drain. The patch of mold above our fridge has taken on a 666 shape. Last Sunday after church, everyone discovered that their copy of the Book of Mormon had been replaced with a Brian Evenson novel."

"I swear, I smell sulfur in the halls now, in addition to the tobacco smoke."

Lund reported that her roommate recently awoke just in time to see a dark figure fleeing from her bedside. "We think it was an incubus, which we know about because Incubus is our favorite rock group. Now she has this really rare STD, but she swears she hasn't been with anybody for, like, several weeks."

Lund said she hopes to find another apartment "before this place gets sucked down to hell like Carrie's house. If only BYU hadn't forsaken us!"

Views from the Street

Brigham Young University has renewed its emphasis against bare midriffs. What do you think?

"It's a woman's responsibility not to tempt men, while being sexy enough to make me want to marry her and have babies."

"I think we should just start pretending that none of us have any naked parts, ever, anywhere."

"If the girls all cover up, who are we going to blame for our impure thoughts and actions?"

"Well, it makes more sense than the rule against beards. After all, Brigham Young never appeared in public with a bare midriff."

"While they're at it, I hope they'll do something to keep plumber's butt where it belongs: on hairy, fat, middle-aged men."

"The guys keep asking me if I'm cold and if I could use some Spackle in the back. What's that supposed to mean?"

Corrections

A feature in last week's entertainment guide gave incorrect dates for performances of Nathaniel Patterson's one-man show at BYU's Margetts Theatre. "*I Am Mormon: A Night of Interpretive Dance and Whimsy*" will be performed Thursday, Friday, and Saturday beginning at 3:00 p.m.

Last issue, an article about a BYU bishopric's plan to use polygraph tests during temple recommend interviews misspelled the surname of the criminal investigator who advised the stake presidency on the matter. He is Frank von Hippel, not von Hipple.

An article about BYU physicist Hyrum Wheeler in last issue's science section misstated the date of a symposium exploring his research. His theory of symmetries in 1-plus-1 dimensional space-time and the operation of the Holy Ghost will be presented on April 24.

Chapter 4:
Ye Elders of Israel

Ah, the men of the church. The priesthood. The brethren, with a lowercased B (for upper case, you have to be a General Authority). If you've spent more than five seconds in a Mormon priesthood meeting, you have sung a hymn called "Ye Elders of Israel," with lyrics by the excellently named Cyrus H. Wheelock. This hymn is apparently the default hymn for any gathering of men in the church. Unless someone specifies something else, "Ye Elders of Israel" will be sung with manly gusto.

This hymn includes the line, "*O Babylon, O Babylon, we bid thee farewell; we're going to the mountains of Ephraim to dwell.*" Addressing Babylon directly, in the context of bidding it farewell, seems like an odd thing to do. If you're really going to leave Babylon, why would you bother to tell it goodbye? But anyway, we have found much to cover among the Elders of Israel in the mountains of Ephraim, Utah, and beyond. In fact, this is the book's longest chapter. Hmm, what does that signify?

Man's Addiction to Wife Destroying Relationship with Porn

By Teancum Zenos Smoot IV

AUSTIN, TX—After years of commitment and fidelity, Austin resident Jesse Bingham is watching his relationship with porn be torn apart by his raging addiction to his wife.

"I never thought it would happen to me," said Bingham, sitting in an apartment rife with the telltale signs of wife addiction: photographs, love letters, gifts. "My relationship with my porn was a deep one. I only had eyes for the girls in the magazines, the videos, or on the Internet, but then, one day. . . ."

According to sources close to Bingham, his descent into wife addiction started innocently enough. "He just went to a dance," said Torvald Hampton, a college buddy. "It wasn't like he was pursuing an addiction to a real live woman. He was just curious. But once he had a taste, he just couldn't keep away."

Hampton recounted numerous nights spent watching porn videos alone in his apartment while his once-faithful friend was out feeding the bottomless pit of his new addiction. "Man, sometimes he just went too far, bringing Nancy right into the apartment here. I mean, what was I supposed to do? He'd sit there on the couch—the very couch where we first watched *Bilious Lesbian Circus Vendors*—and put his arm around her waist!"

Bingham's psychologist, with permission from Bingham, says he shows all the signs of a deepening spouse addiction. "He spent all his money on her. He neglected his magazines, missed his weekly visits to the Hentai Hut of Hooters, and started getting up in the middle of the night to write e-mails to his beloved. I tell you, it's a classic case."

More disturbing still are accounts from Bingham's family that he actually started showing signs of caring about the woman who would, one dark day, become his wife. "He took care of her for a whole week while she was sick," said Sara Bingham, Jesse's younger sister. "Took leave from work and everything. She threw up on him, which should have given him a clue. But no. Jesse was too far gone by then. What kind of expectation is he setting for me here?"

"I have unrealistic expectations for my porn now, and it just can't live up to those."

Bingham admits that he is completely enveloped by his addiction to his wife. "I think about her constantly. I go home to her every chance I get. I've barely seen my porn since my wife addiction started. And when I do . . . I don't know, the trust just isn't there anymore, you know? But the fact is, my wife has set the standard too high. I have unrealistic expectations for my porn now, and it just can't live up to those."

Bingham swears he has tried to go back to

his porn, "but I just expect all these perverse things, like warmth, flirtation, care, and an actual female body, and my porn just cannot put out."

Bingham and his porn are on a trial separation to see if they can work out their differences. His porn has gone to Hampton's apartment for the duration of the separation.

Priesthood Holder Redoubles His Efforts
By Jack B. Kimball

DURANGO, CO—Local elder Daniel Pierson recently realized that the only thing he's used his priesthood for during the past three years is choosing who says the blessing on the food.

"I've got to get myself back up to peak spiritual power," he says. "I've gotten lax, just rotating among my kids instead of pausing for inspiration to find out who heaven really wants to say the prayer."

Pierson hopes that more opportunities to use the priesthood come his way soon. "I'm not saying I want someone to get sick or anything," he says. "But the next time the quorum gets assigned to stack the chairs, I'm definitely going to participate."

Miracle Expedites Home Teaching
By Jack B. Kimball

BURLEY, ID—Area man Richard Cranney reported that he and his companion achieved one-hundred-percent home teaching last month under miraculous circumstances.

"I sat down with the phone on a Thursday evening," Cranney said. "I called all four families and got the head of the household on the first try. No busy signals, no answering machines, no snotty kids. What's more, all the families agreed to consecutive appointments. To top it off, when I called my companion to tell him the great news, I got him on the second ring and he had no scheduling conflicts."

Cranney said that he believes the kingdom's work is being hastened in these last days.

Area Man Takes Sabbath Sabbatical
By Jack B. Kimball

BOCA RATON, FL—Local member Doug Whitehead announced that from now on, he will be staying home on the last Sunday of every month to "refresh my spiritual palate." Whitehead said he would use his "Sabbath sabbath" to sleep, catch up on DVDs and magazines, and do other relaxing things.

"My home teaching companion is gonna have to get used to making appointments on the second-to-last Sunday of the month," Whitehead said. His wife is trying to convince him to spend his Sabbath sabbaths doing something religiously productive at home, such as inventorying the food storage.

In addition to Sabbath sabbaths, Whitehead said he is considering taking a yearlong sabbatical from church activity every seventh year.

quieter quorum members better. "You know, like Car-Crash-Victim-Looking Guy," he said. "I want to know what his deal is." However, he expressed reservations about certain other members. "Some of them I'm not sure I have anything in common with," he admitted. "Like that one guy, Freaky Eyes Who Bought His Mattress at DI. The one who keeps flirting with Old-Lady-Lookin' Girl. I hear he's pretty weird. I guess inspiration will help me learn to love them all, though."

Elders Quorum President Claims Empathy as Biggest Asset

By Kylee-Ashlee Cannon Christiansen

HIGHLAND, UT—Steve Hammond, the newly called elders quorum president of the Highland Sixty-Sixth Ward, cites his "deep and personal love" for his quorum members as his greatest talent.

"You really have to care about each member in your charge and know him personally in order to succeed in this calling," Hammond said. "And I have to say that I enjoy lots of good personal relationships with this quorum. Like with Brother Whatshisname. I call him Rug Boy because of his toupee. He nods and smiles at me almost every week."

Hammond is already thinking about his potential counselors. "That one guy, the one who looks like the Pillsbury Doughboy, the guy who's married to Huge-Breasted Redhead, he'd probably make a good counselor, I guess," Hammond said. "He certainly dresses the part. And I know him pretty well since that time we chatted at the ward Christmas party." Hammond is also considering either Surfer Dude or Mr. Sieg Heil Scout Leader as possible counselors.

As quorum president, Hammond is looking forward to getting to know some of the

Hammond is considering either Surfer Dude or Mr. Sieg Heil Scout Leader as possible counselors.

Despite the anticipated difficulties, Hammond is grateful for the calling. "It's cool that Bishop Smooth Talkin' Business Man wanted me to do this," he said. "You know, the guy who sits on the stand every week and is married to the lady you wouldn't guess had sex, except she's got kids. Or maybe he's married to Sister Salad-and-Water. Whatever. Anyway, he's a pretty cool guy."

Poll Reveals Majority of Men "Highly Satisfied" with Patriarchy

By Lisa Layton

PROVO, UT—In a recent phone poll of 582 Mormon men conducted by the Society for the Advancement of Patriarchy (SAP), seventy-nine percent said they were "highly satisfied" with patriarchy, citing such personal benefits as "power," "respect," and "being part of a tradition."

Among those who stated they were only "satisfied," most said the benefits of patriarchy were a tradeoff for the responsibility of being lord and master of a home. A SAP spokesman stated that no equivalent poll of Mormon women is planned.

Gospel Doctrine Instructor Breaks Post-Question Silence Record

KILLEEN, TX—Karl Stevens, a Gospel Doctrine teacher in the Killeen Second Ward, broke the post-question silence record last week by asking his Sunday school class the following question: "What exactly happened to Lot's wife?" After forty minutes of silence, Sister Carole Anne Walker rose and offered the closing prayer.

The previous record of thirty-seven minutes was held by Stephen Johansen of Fairbanks, Alaska, who asked for an explanation of Isaiah 1:13, which reads: *"Bring no more vain oblations; incense is an abomination unto me; the new moons and sabbaths, the calling of assemblies, I cannot away with; it is iniquity, even the solemn meeting."*

Provo Man Votes Democrat "Just to See What It Feels Like"

By Jack B. Kimball

PROVO, UT—Area resident Scott Nibley has never felt tempted by the Democrats before, having always punched the straight Republican ticket. However, when he faced down his blank ballot during the recent election, he was overcome with a sudden rush of carnal desire to see what it would feel like to punch Democrat.

"I figured nobody would have to know, and if it was only this one time I'd be forgiven," Nibley said. "I did feel a rush of freedom and rebellion, but afterwards I couldn't look my folks in the eye. I felt dirty, even after a fifteen-minute shower."

In order to facilitate his repentance, Nibley volunteered to join the city's post-election cleanup crew. "I especially focused on taking down the Democrat signs," he said. "They're like political pornography."

Boston Resident Finally Convinces Coworkers He Has Only One Wife

By Terrill W. Cannon

JAMAICA PLAIN, MA—After years of failed attempts to proselytize his coworkers, Nathan Huffhinds has finally convinced four of his fellow CPAs that he has only one wife. "It's taken years," he said. "I've even had Leanne come in on more than one occasion, but it didn't seem to have any effect."

Huffhinds finally persuaded them by pointing out that the tax benefits of having more than one spouse are nil. "The marriage penalty is bad enough as it is," Huffhinds said. "Could you imagine that times five, ten, fifteen?" Huffhinds considers this a small but important victory for the church. "I was glad for the opportunity."

Seminary Teacher Unveils New Doctrine

By Kylee-Ashlee Cannon Christiansen

HYRUM, UT—Popular Hyrum High School seminary teacher Thoyd K. Dowdle denies that he is "heaven's holy conduit for these days," as some of his students claim, and says that he is just a "simple and humble" seminary teacher.

"I just want to preach the gospel in peace," he says.

However, McDowdle's startlingly deep understanding of the scriptures began to garner attention soon after he started teaching in Hyrum. In only his first year, McDowdle revealed a brand-new doctrine that electrified his students.

"He told me that when we die, Moroni, Christopher Columbus, Thomas Moore, and all these other guys will bow down to worship us because we lived in the days of President Hinckley," said Daniel Howe, a former student who has given up a scholarship to the University of Utah to study the scriptures at McDowdle's side. "I mean, how cool is that?"

McDowdle's extraordinary revelations include explaining that the scriptural whore of Babylon is actually Paris Hilton.

McDowdle is the first to teach this new doctrine. "I'd never heard that before, and I couldn't find it in the scriptures or any of the general conference *Ensign*s," said Laetitia Hopkins, a senior in McDowdle's class. "So obviously this must have been revealed directly to Brother McDowdle. Also, he told me that I'd better go out with Curt Hale."

McDowdle's other extraordinary acts include:

- Interpreting several of his class members' patriarchal blessings
- Twice casting demons out of his classroom
- Prophesying a 7.4 earthquake for Southern California unless Hollywood repents
- Seeing visions of particular students who would "stray" during prom
- Explaining that the scriptural whore of Babylon is actually Paris Hilton

Laetitia Hopkins is currently conducting a letter campaign to get McDowdle considered for a General Authority position. "Brother McDowdle must have some kind of special relationship with heaven," she said, "because how could anyone make this stuff up?"

High Councilman Calls Eleventh Article of Faith "No Longer Relevant"

By Lisa Layton

PIMA, AZ—In a recent talk to the Pima Fourth Ward, high councilman Preston Bryce warned members not to be led astray by too much emphasis on the eleventh Article of Faith, which states, "We claim the privilege of worshipping according to the dictates of our own conscience, and allow all men the same privilege, let them worship, how, where, or what they may."

"Sometimes people use the eleventh Article of Faith as an excuse to refrain from doing missionary work," Bryce said from the pulpit. "They say, 'I don't want to force my beliefs and opinions on the people I live and work with. My friends and neighbors know what I believe, and if they're interested, they'll come ask me.' But that attitude doesn't really fit in with our ideas about missionary work, brothers and sisters."

Bryce explained that the eleventh Article of Faith was necessary in the early days, when the church faced oppression and had

not converted millions of people to the truth. "But now that the truthfulness of the gospel is accepted by so many people, that particular Article of Faith is no longer relevant in the ways it once was."

Reaction to the talk was mixed. Local member Marge Pepper stated, "I definitely felt inspired as Brother Bryce was talking. I have always been bothered by the eleventh Article of Faith. First of all, it doesn't start with 'We believe' like all the others, and I never could see why we should just let everyone else believe whatever they want when we know the church is true. It would be better if we just got rid of it—after all, twelve is a much nicer number than unlucky thirteen."

Roger and Joan Cannon, on the other hand, both expressed concern over the message. "I thought free agency was central to the gospel," Joan said. "It's as if he's forgotten the story of the War in Heaven, where it was decided we all needed to be able to choose what we accept."

"It would be better if we just got rid of it—after all, twelve is a much nicer number than unlucky thirteen."

"What's Brother Bryce going to do, anyway?" her husband Roger asked. "Write to the Brethren and ask them to delete that passage from the scriptures?"

Upon hearing of such objections, Bryce dismissed them. "My talk has nothing in common with Satan's plan in the preexistence. Remember, Satan was evil and wanted to thwart the plan of salvation, while I am simply trying to help accomplish the plan in the most straightforward way possible. After all, I did say that we shouldn't force anyone to be Mormon."

LDS Man Proposes Ecclesiastical IRAs

By Terrill W. Cannon

ST. GEORGE, UT—For some time Bill Kelly, an investment specialist from St. George, has been wondering when the Republicans are going to offer a tax break to all those faithful who are struggling under the yoke of fiscal responsibilities to their churches.

"If Mormons really are the chosen people on this continent, then where's our tax break?" says Kelly. "We get a little break on our tithing and fast offerings, but it's in the form of a deduction, not a tax credit like big business gets."

Kelly says that he's seen the writing on the wall. "I've been calling [Orrin] Hatch for the last two years, trying to get something done, but it seems like business as usual. We're not going to get a tax break, but maybe we could get a tax shelter."

As Kelly likes to point out, Mormons are now the most likely group of people to go bankrupt. "Additionally," he says, "Mormons have the fifth-worse per-capita income in the country." Kelly argues that this is not because of tithing or large families but because of a "regressive tax code" that penalizes people for their religious affiliations.

"In America, we show what we value by the kinds of tax-free accounts we create," Kelly says. "We value health care, and viola—we get medical savings accounts. We value education, and voila—we get educational IRAs. We value leisure, and voila—we get the mutual fund and the capital growth account. It seems clear to me from looking at the availability of our financial products that America doesn't value religion."

According to Kelly, if America did value religion, the legislature would allow for an ecclesiastical IRA that would let God-fearing Americans keep their money tax-free for the paying of tithing, fast offerings, and mission expenses. "And why doesn't it happen?" Kelly asks. "Because Washington is a pit of Molech worshippers who want to bleed religious people dry and give all our money to indigents."

> **"Washington is a pit of Molech worshippers who want to bleed religious people dry and give all our money to indigents."**

A pamphlet Kelly has been circulating argues that "we are to render unto Caesar that which is Caesar's and do likewise unto heaven. Under the current system, we are unable to do that. Because of paycheck withholding, we must render unto Caesar before we can render unto the church. The ecclesiastical IRA will let us keep heaven's ten percent out of the government's hands, where we may or may not ever get it back."

Jaynelle Davenport, a retiree, has been reading Kelly's materials, and she is interested. "Once again we see the rich being penalized for being rich," she says. "I'm sick of taxes that don't go for anything I'm interested in. I'd like to see that tax money go for temples or institute buildings. It looks like an ecclesiastical IRA is the way to go for me and my dead husband's pension money."

Kelly says that if he can get the legislature to recognize the true spirit of this American continent by passing ecclesiastical IRA legislation, then he'd be ready to start signing people up and rolling over the money from their traditional and Roth IRAs. "I'll only charge a ten-percent commission, no more nor less than the kingdom itself asks for," says Kelly. "I really want to get this country back to its religious roots, and this seems like the way to do it. It's a win-win-win situation."

Gay Polygamists Make Bid for Legitimacy

CAMBRIDGE, MA—In a bold move, Latter-day Saints who are both homosexual and polygamist have banded together to lobby for greater acceptance and understanding. Called Poly-Gay-Mists Now and Forever, the advocacy group has begun holding rallies, seminars, love-ins, and weddings in Massachusetts, with events planned soon for locations in California and Utah.

"My Heavenly Father created me to love men, and not just one," said Daniel Bryant, a sixth-generation Mormon who grew up in Centerville, Utah, and now lives in Somerville, Massachusetts, where he serves as editor of the group's newsletter, *Come, All Ye Sons of God.* "I am a gay fundamentalist who believes in Joseph Smith's original teachings regarding the plurality of partners, and I believe that extends to same-gender relationships. We're trying to be true to our feelings as well as our heritage."

Howard Brooks, founder of the Poly-Gay-Mist movement, would not speak directly to reporters. The *Enquirer* has learned, however, that Brooks grew up in a fundamentalist polygamist family in Colorado City, Arizona.

Leaving home at age seventeen, he departed from the faith's teachings for several decades. Two years ago, he became reconverted to fundamentalist beliefs, but by then he was already irrevocably gay. Today, Brooks is eternally sealed to three men. Under the Poly-Gay-Mist bylaws, all husbands within a family group may freely fraternize with one another.

"This merging of two Mormon subcultures is unexpected but strangely inevitable," said Eric Newberry, a University of Utah sociologist. "It's as if the two opposite ends of the spectrum curved around and met in the rear, so to speak. If this catches on, it could help alleviate the extreme competition for females among fundamentalist Mormons."

"We're trying to be true to our feelings as well as our heritage."

George Welch, spokesman for the National Association for the Advancement of Polygamists (NAAP), said, "While the Poly-Gay-Mists are not a traditional polygamist group, we nevertheless embrace them with open arms, and they're welcome to have a booth at our NAAP convention in October. In fact, we hope they'll queer-eye some of the other booths that could use a little more pizzazz."

For more information about Poly-Gay-Mists Now and Forever, visit www.multiple-husbands.org.

Dutton, who was raised Mormon, has not attended church since he was in high school. "I have these home teachers and missionaries coming by all the time. We used to lay low until they left, but I tell you what. Next time I'm going to let them fellas come in and talk."

Nevada Man Wrecks Truck to Avoid the Appearance of Evil
By Terrill W. Cannon

TONOPAH, NV—While on the southern run from Ely to Reno, long-distance trucker Homer Dutton spotted a lone figure in a tuxedo, standing in the middle of the westbound lane. The figure's arm was extended, "and he was pointing right at me," Dutton says.

Dutton swerved abruptly, his rig skidding off the highway and eventually coming to a stop in a small cluster of Joshua trees. Although he sustained no injuries, the flat iron he was hauling is now scattered across the desert.

"It scared the pants off me, I tell you," Dutton said. "One minute there was open road, and the next this fella was just standing there in my headlights, laughing. I didn't have time to honk or nothing. I just reefed on that wheel and ditched. You can see folks like that in Vegas, broke gamblers out trying to sober up. But there's no tuxedo gambling in Tonopah, just video poker, slots, and the whorehouses. It's weird, man."

Dutton said the figure stood in the road watching him as he climbed out of his truck. "He had these glowing white eyes, and I swear, you're not going to believe this, but he had chicken feet sticking out of them pant legs."

At that point, Dutton said, he dropped to his knees and started praying. "I was blubbering and crying like a baby."

"That man was pure evil. I hate to think what would have happened if I'd of run him over."

Police found no trace of the chicken-footed man, though Dutton swears he saw him heading for town. "That man was pure evil. There's no doubt in my mind. I hate to think what would have happened if I'd of run him over. There'd be hell to pay, for sure."

Area Man Still Unsure about Church Policy on Porn
By Jack B. Kimball

EAGER, AZ—After listening to general conference, Ted Yates expressed dismay that the church still hasn't clarified its position regarding the pornography that's so widely available today.

"I mean, we know we're not supposed to gamble or drink coffee, but what about all these nudie pictures available on the Internet?" he asked. "It seems like this is an important enough deal that the church would give us some clear guidance. Some of the General Authorities have alluded to this issue, but they just haven't come out with anything definitive yet."

Know Your Mormon Terms

Outer Parkness: Where church members go who are slothful about getting to their meetings on time

Ward Clerk Reads Priesthood Lesson in Advance

OGDEN, UT—Tim Bogert, ward clerk for the Ogden Fourteenth Ward, reported that he read a lesson from the priesthood manual a week in advance. "Yes, I'm afraid I really did," said Bogert. "I think it was about following the brethren, or another topic like obedience maybe."

Bogert admitted that he felt guilty about reading the lesson. "I wasn't sure if it was something I was allowed to do, so I made an appointment to discuss it with Bishop Beck. He was very understanding and listened to all my misgivings. We even went through the handbook of instructions, and nothing in there said you couldn't read the lesson in advance. So I figured I was okay."

James Page, professor of history at Utah State University, said he isn't sure it is a good idea to read the manual in advance. "I mean, numerous studies have shown that the teacher will have to come up with his own insights and tell personal experiences if he can't just call on people in class to read straight out of the manual."

Page, whose Ph.D. dissertation was on the history of church manual layouts and graphic arts, continued: "Look, if everyone reads the manual, they'll want to discuss the topics, and I'm not sure that's a good idea."

Views from the Street

What are you doing to prepare for eventual hardships or disasters?

"I live next door to the stake canning director, so I'm practicing my half-starved look."

"To conserve precious hygienic resources, I no longer use toothpaste, soap, or deodorant."

"As for me and my house, we're all well-trained in semi-automatic weapon usage."

"I bought 100 white shirts, so I can continue exercising the priesthood after the demise of the clothing and laundry industries."

"I've stockpiled three extra boxes of mac and cheese."

"What? I thought all this talk of food storage was just a spiritual metaphor."

Former Clerk Experiences Miracle of Tithing

By Milton P. Romney

AMMON, ID—When former Ammon Thirty-Third Ward financial clerk Gavin Keebler was required to pay back most of the money he stole from his ward's accounts, he was pretty sure it would cause a financial setback from which his family would never recover. Fortunately for Keebler, he never lost his faith.

Keebler was sentenced this month to pay restitution in the amount of 90 percent of what he embezzled. According to court records, that amounted to $63,000 of the $70,000 he stole over the course of three years.

"The other $7,000 I had already paid back to the church," explains Keebler. "I carefully accounted for all the money I took and paid an honest tithe." Now he believes he has reaped the rewards for his faithfulness.

"I wrote out the restitution check for the full amount, not having any idea where the money would come from," says Keebler, "but the check cleared, and when I looked in my account, I still had nearly $60,000!"

Keebler claims there is no way to account for the money other than a tithing miracle, since most of what he originally took had already been spent on a new Land Rover and a golf cart that looks like a Humvee.

Shari Keebler, his wife of eighteen years, recalls the day. "We were so scared," she said. "We had written that check knowing full well we didn't have enough money, but our faith was sufficient, and now Gavin is clear, and we have money in the bank we had never planned on, plus the Land Rover! Heaven has surely blessed us!"

"Generally, we don't allow filthy lucre to be tithed, but obviously in this case we weren't aware of what this clerk was doing."

Church authorities are slow to attribute the miracle to the blessings of tithing. Bishop Ron Anderson of the Thirty-Third Ward said, "Generally, we don't allow filthy lucre to be tithed, but obviously in this case we weren't aware of what Gavin was doing. Any blessings he received as a result of this aren't really his, and he should probably consider returning them to the church."

Keebler says he has no intention of doing so. "I paid that tithing in good faith, believing it was what the Lord would have me do," he said. "I prefer to think of this as the windows of heaven pouring forth."

Know Your Mormon Terms

Melchizedork: Adult men who wear shorts with their garments hanging out below the hem

Coffee Rumor Ruins Investment Firm

By Milton P. Romney

REXBURG, ID—The small brokerage firm of Pratt & Cooper faced ruin last week when investors were led to believe that one of the firm's principals could not be trusted to invest wisely. The subsequent deluge of requests for withdrawal by panicked local investors sent Pratt & Cooper into bankruptcy.

According to former client Mrs. Harold M. Prescott, the alarm was sounded when she happened into the office early last Monday morning. "I came in to discuss a couple of trades I was considering," reports Mrs. Prescott, "when I noticed the Java Express cup on Mr. Cooper's desk. It was terrifying to me—terrifying—to think that this man was attempting to assist me with my investment portfolio and yet was not availing himself of the Spirit!" Prescott transferred all her accounts to another firm that very morning.

Word of Alma Cooper's spiritual violation spread quickly through this small town as visiting teaching calling chains went into action. "We felt this could potentially affect enough of our members that we began call-

ing people immediately," said Trudy Nelson, president of the Twelfth Ward Relief Society. "It is beyond comprehension how reckless he was being with our money!" By that afternoon, Pratt & Cooper had lost seventy-three percent of its holdings and was on the verge of collapsing.

Despite concerted efforts to notify the public that the offending beverage was nothing but a Chocolate Steamer, Java Express's name for hot chocolate made with the steamed milk popularized by espresso drinks, it was too late to restore client confidence. "We even took the cup to an independent testing company, which verified that there was nothing wicked in that cup," said Sam Thompson, an intern who is presently looking for work. "I guess if there's a lesson to be learned in all of this, it's to follow the counsel of the church in avoiding the very appearance of evil."

Many previous clients remained dismayed despite the news that there was no coffee in the cup. "Regardless of what he was drinking, he exercised incredibly poor judgment," said Ralph Mortensen. "He looks pretty good all wrapped up in that wool suit of his, but how do we know what's really on the inside now? Point is, we don't know, and I don't plan on finding out the hard way."

Alma Cooper, though unavailable for comment, was heard by witnesses to admit that in the future, he would take his chocolate milk cold.

First Husband Prevails in Landmark Case

By Milton P. Romney

HEAVEN—In what is being called a precedent-setting case, the Honorable Judge Abijah, son of Joseph, son of Jacob, acting in his role as chief judge of the Tribe of Ephraim in Heaven, ruled last week in favor of Elbert Huntington, deceased since 1935 and first husband of Elenora Huntington Armiston. Judge Abijah ruled that even though Brother Huntington never sired any children by his wife before being killed in an unfortunate accident involving a herd of cattle and a slingshot, he is legally entitled to eternal custody rights to all of Sister Armiston's children by her second husband, Eugene Armiston.

"Inasmuch as Brother Huntington was a faithful, if not all that bright, husband for six short weeks prior to his untimely demise, and in that time he did nothing to diminish his worthiness regarding the blessings of the holy sealing committed in the St. George Temple on the day of his wedding," reads the judge's decision, "it is appropriate in mine eyes that he retain all the blessings of that sealing, including rightful eternal parenthood to all progeny that sprung from the loins of his rightful wife."

From his mansion in East Moronihahburg on a planet near Kolob, Brother Huntington declared, "This is a great day for all first hus-

bands. My wife, tramp that she turned out to be, is still mine by covenant, and the courts of heaven have vindicated me today by granting me the children that never knew me." He intends now to pursue legal action ensuring that his wife's sealing ordinance to Armiston also be revoked, thereby returning her, forcibly if necessary, to her rightful place as a "handmaiden in my little kingdom of heaven, where she belongs."

"All her kids, spiritual or otherwise, are mine now anyway," Huntington claims, "so I might just as well be the one fathering those kids through the eternities." He said he was pleased to note that the blueprints for her resurrected body indicate a return to the weight and bust-size she possessed when he married her, but he claims that had no bearing on his decision.

> ## Huntington is pleased that the blueprints for his wife's resurrected body indicate a return to the weight and bust-size she possessed when he married her.

An appeal is expected. Thomas L. Card, the attorney representing Sister Armiston and her second husband, Eugene Armiston (deceased since 1981), indicated in a press conference that every reasonable effort would be made to change the will of the court in this matter. "These children are the eternal progeny of Eugene Armiston. Period," he said. "Brother Huntington would have plenty of opportunity to meet other available deceased women who would be happy to bear him spirit children if he would just get on with his life after death."

Despite the controversy, Brother Huntington is getting to know his deceased daughter and watching the living children from on high, trying to learn all their names.

Man Dials Wrong Number, Gets Mormons Instead of Hot Babes

FARGO, ND—Area resident Frank O'Brian found that he was the victim of either a faulty memory or supernatural promptings when he called 1-900-Hot-Babes early Tuesday morning.

Having been lured into dialing the number for Hot Babes by a late-night television ad depicting scantily clad women wielding firearms, O'Brian dialed a number on his telephone. Expecting a pleasant conversation with a hot babe, O'Brian was surprised when a representative of the church asked if he wanted the Bible or the Book of Mormon.

"I thought them was weird names for girls," said O'Brian, breaking open a beer in front of two youthful male missionaries. "But when the lady said she'd send 'em right over, I just asked for both."

O'Brian admitted that he was further pleased when the person on the other end of the line asked if he wanted a free video as well.

"How could I refuse?" asked O'Brian, turning *Our Heavenly Father's Plan* over in his hands, which he admitted was not quite what he expected. "Do you kids make much money at this?" he asked the missionaries.

Spokesmen deny that the church is using any innovative television campaigns that may have confused O'Brian. "Maybe Brother O'Brian was dialing the number while one of our ads was playing on his television," speculated Elder Dwight, one of the missionaries who delivered the books and video.

"I think the Spirit guided him," said Elder Murray, the senior companion of the duo, as he waved O'Brian's tobacco smoke away from his face.

The missionaries refused the videos that O'Brian offered to lend them. "I figured one good turn deserves another," he said.

Utah Man Calls Jewish Neighbor "Gentile"
By Terrill W. Cannon

PROVO, UT—When L. Tyree Smedley, a lifetime resident of Utah County, visited his new neighbors, Harvey and Sheila Goldstein, he informed them that "gentiles" sometimes find it hard to adjust to the religious climate of Utah. An ex-marine, Goldstein said he'd been called every horrible name in the book, "heeb, kike, you name it, but never in fifty-five years have I been called a gentile. It was kind of amazing."

Goldstein and his wife laughed so hard that a disgruntled Brother Smedley whistled for the dog and returned to his house. "We felt bad about that," said Mrs. Goldstein. "I'm going to bake him a challah and take it over. It was rude of us to laugh at someone who obviously had no idea what he was saying." Mr. Goldstein hastened to add, "But we really couldn't help it."

Area Men Recover from Annual Mother's Day Self-Flagellation Rituals

By Kylee-Ashlee Cannon Christiansen

LINDON, UT—The men of the Lindon Hills Forty-Third Ward are still exhausted from their rigorous Mother's Day celebrations. "We try to go the extra mile in showing our wives and mothers how much they mean to us and how utterly unworthy we are to even be in their presence," explained Bishop Bob Creeley. "It's a day of cleansing the soul and of intense groveling for us men."

The sacrament meeting program started out with a talk by Brother Hugh Castleton, the high priest group leader. "My mother tended a half-acre vegetable garden, raised ten children on $15,000 a year, made all our clothes by hand, memorized the entire Book of Mormon, and maintained a perfect size-six figure her entire life," sobbed Brother Castleton. "She taught herself to play the piano after she went blind at age thirty-four, just so she could say yes to the calling of Primary pianist. Using Braille and the Holy Spirit, she made us all pieced quilts for each of our birthdays. I'll never forget watching her pray over her quilting frame, waiting for the Spirit to guide her needle to just the right spot."

Brother Larry Schoendyke presented a moving tribute to his mother. "My mother's last words to me were, 'Larry, everyone is a child of God and deserves to be trusted,'" he recalled. "Two hours later, she was shot and killed by criminals disguised as Jehovah's Witnesses, whom she had invited in for cocoa and homemade cookies. But I'll never forget that wonderful lesson she taught me about trust. What a saint."

Brother Schoendyke's talk was followed by a musical interlude. The Sackcloth-and-Ashes Quartet, made up of four male ward members, sang a song they wrote themselves called "I'm Just a Stupid Man But Please Allow Me to Worship at the Altar of Motherhood."

> ## "I won't interfere with all that holy motherhood stuff. It truly is much more special than we men could ever understand."

The last man to speak on motherhood was Brother Rick Dalmonico, a new father. "Sometimes when I come home and my wife is nursing our newborn, the spirit is so strong that I feel it would be irreverent to interrupt them," he confessed. "So I just usually go in the other room and watch football. I wouldn't want to interfere with something as sacred as precious motherhood." He added, "Or sometimes I just stay out late with friends instead of coming home so I won't interfere with all that holy motherhood stuff. It truly is much more special than we men could ever understand."

After sacrament meeting, the men of the ward adjourned to the foyer, where they covered their heads, donned black robes, and greeted the women on their knees. When the first woman appeared, they prostrated themselves on the ground and chanted "Miserere Mei" several times.

"We know we're just men and therefore the only socially acceptable butt of jokes in the LDS culture," Bishop Creeley said to the women. "We're also aware that we're not entitled to the holy role of mother or even to loosen your sandal straps—we love your sandals, by the way, and you should buy as many more pairs as you want—but please do accept this small token of our worshipfulness, gratitude, and awe."

The men then presented the mothers with large bouquets of roses tied with ribbons that said We're Not Worthy in two-inch letters. Each message had been individually written in the men's own blood the previous Sunday in their elders quorum and high priest groups. "I finally had to nick an artery to get enough blood, and I actually passed out twice," said Brother Craig Davis, describing the ordeal. "But I know my small trial was nothing compared to the travails of laboring to bring a child into the world, which my sweet, dear wife has done twice now, without any pain medication." He added, "She actually recited psalms instead of screaming. What a woman."

Now that the men of the Lindon Hills Forty-Third ward have undergone their annual purge of unworthiness, "we can all get back to important man stuff," admits Brother Schoendyke. He denies rumors that he told his friend he can now ignore his wife in good conscience for another year.

Snapshot

What are we bringing to our home teaching families?

The still-beating hearts of the last family that stood us up

Our wife, because we can't stand our sniveling assigned companion

101 ways to say, "I'd love to help, but I'm really busy"

Bitterness and rancor thinly disguised as a lesson on forgiveness

Herpes

That hidden camera the bishop wants us to plant

The gospel, fellowship, compassion, and the Amway opportunity

The philosophies of men, mingled with obscure Jedediah M. Grant sermons

Blood atonement

The Sports Illustrated swimsuit issue, in a plain brown wrapper, after we've finished with it

Cheez-Whiz

Hofmann Forges Letters from Self

By Teancum Zenos Smoot IV

BLUFFDALE, UT—Adding to the web of lies and deceit that landed Mark Hofmann in prison two decades ago, authorities have recently discovered that Hofmann has been forging letters ostensibly from himself and sending them to his friends and relatives.

"As is typical of Hofmann, he has taken every precaution to make the letters seem utterly real," said Sergeant Jack Molin, a forensics specialist with the Salt Lake City Police Department.

Samples of the ink from many of Hofmann's alleged letters have been traced directly to a pen in the Utah State Prison that bears Hofmann's fingerprints. Traces of his DNA have even been found on the counterfeit letters.

"Mark has definitely outdone himself," said Mormon historian John Harrington. "Not even the infamous white salamander letter that fooled the whole church can stack up

to the expertise of these forgeries. I've heard that he even managed to get a hold of the sheaf of paper he keeps in his cell to forge the letters on."

Even Dan Lafferty, Hofmann's famous cellmate, didn't know that Hofmann was up to his old mischief. Lafferty claims Hofmann hasn't broken from his normal routine of reading books, lifting weights, and writing.

"How could I know he was actually forging his own handwriting when I thought he was innocently writing a letter? He never even hinted about it," said Lafferty

Some of the recipients of Hofmann's now-debunked missives express a sense of having been betrayed. "It's amazing," said Harold Cracken, who used to serve on a ward activities committee with Hofmann. "The writing looked like his, and the tone of the letter sounded like the Mark I thought I knew. But now I find out it's all fake. Mark is just a mystery to me now."

"As is typical of Hofmann, he has taken every precaution to make the letters seem utterly real."

Discovery of the letters' falsity has destroyed the plans of at least one investor. Greg Moorehead has been collecting Hofmann's letters quietly for some years, hoping to sell them to historical societies, libraries, or even the LDS Church itself. But now that the world knows they're forgeries, the letters' only value lies in their oddity.

Additionally, this sudden flood of forgeries has made the bottom drop out of the Mormon forgery market. "I can barely finagle five dollars apiece out of Benchmark Book for all these letters now," said Moorehead. "And they're always trying to give it to me in used book credit."

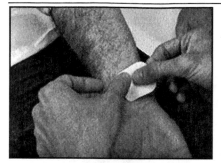

New Patch Magnifies Priesthood

By Milton P. Romney

TWIN FALLS, ID—Personal Priesthood, Inc., recently announced the release of the Priesthood Enlargement Patch (PEP), designed to magnify the priesthood of all male members.

Based on a secret combination of herbs, consecrated oils, and spiritual incantations, the PEP is touted as the first of its kind. "Many of our brethren are insecure about the abilities of their priesthood," said PPI executive Eric T. "Big" Johnson. "PEP makes it possible for the priesthood holder to magnify his calling without lying to himself or others."

Though the product is not intended for use by women, Johnson anticipates that women will constitute an important market demographic. "No one is happier about this product than my wife, who has complained for years about the power of my priesthood," says Johnson.

Snapshot

What are some side effects of the ban on guns in church?

40% fewer deaths at youth basketball games

No more gunpoint sacrament tray hijacks

Disciplinary councils can no longer be settled by duels

Kevlar suit coat sales plummet

Huge decrease in usage of the phrase, "Do you feel lucky, brother? Well, do ya?"

Nursery leader suddenly a much tougher job

Stake Young Men presidency in Columbine, Colorado, lifts ban on Marilyn Manson as fireside speaker

Eagle Forum Mormons wear flag lapel pins sideways, in silent protest

Doctrinal disputes now have to be settled the old-fashioned way: knife fighting

Cemetery groundskeeper notices strange rumbling noises coming from Ezra Taft Benson's grave

In Gartner's case, the bishop thought a little extra preliminary work was required, and he gently but firmly reminded her that if she were performing her wifely duties, her husband wouldn't need to satisfy his intimacy needs elsewhere. "He helped me understand that Richard is hungry, and as he scans the menu I'm not a very appealing entrée," she

Bishop's Formula Saves Marriage

By Milton P. Romney

LAKE OSWEGO, OR—Shannon Gartner thought her marriage of twenty-four years was over when she caught her husband in his sixth extramarital affair in nearly as many years. In a last-ditch effort to salvage her marital covenants, she met with Bishop Brian Peterson, and she credits that experience with saving her marriage.

"Bishop Peterson was very loving," she said with tears gathering in the corners of her eyes. "He knew right away how to fix everything."

Peterson has been the bishop of the Lake View Ward for just under two years, and he says he's seen a lot of these kinds of cases. "The world is full of people who make their lives unnecessarily messy," he says. "Over the years, I've developed a simple formula to solve most of the little problems in my ward. The key is family home evening, regular scripture study, and family prayer. It's pretty much just mathematical. You do the right things, you get the right results."

said. Citing the mantle of his authority, the bishop recommended breast augmentation and some weight loss. "Most importantly, I'm finally getting the picture that this is mostly my fault," Gartner added gratefully.

As is typical when Satan tries to prevent something righteous from occurring, initial efforts to implement the bishop's formula were fraught with difficulty. But Gartner says that patience and longsuffering have paid off and that family home evening, in particular, has been "like a miracle."

"The key is family home evening, regular scripture study, and family prayer. It's pretty much just mathematical."

"Don't misunderstand," she says, "it was hard at first. Our oldest daughter is living with her boyfriend and their infant son, so she's hardly ever available, and the other kids are either out with their friends or on the Internet until all hours of the night. Plus, Bruce has been putting in a lot of overtime at the office again." Gartner credits the decrease in Internet pornography viewed by their teenage sons to family home evening, and she says Bruce now makes some effort to be home from work by 7:30 on Monday nights. "I always bake his favorite brownies to help incentivize him to be there by the opening song."

Scripture study and family prayer proved to be every bit as problematic. "Bishop Peterson made it very clear that I must not usurp Richard's priesthood authority and that I had to find a way to get him to initiate the prayer and scripture reading so it seemed like his idea." She reports that by hiding his liquor, she has managed to cajole him into gathering for prayer on three separate occasions. In each instance, "the spirit was so strong that I just knew our sixth grader, Jason, would eventually overcome his bed-wetting problem."

Now that she has lost five pounds and even colored her hair, Gartner feels more confident than ever that she'll win back her husband's affections for good. "I just know that if I keep at it, I won't ever have to bear the guilt of breaking my temple covenants." Her daughter's boyfriend was recently arrested on drug trafficking charges, so her daughter and grandson will soon be moving home. "This is not just a coincidence," she says with conviction. "We have been so blessed by the wise counsel of our bishop. Family home evening, prayer, and scripture study have literally been the salvation of our little family. And after next week, I'll be a double D!"

Know Your Mormon Terms

Raptism: An immersion by culture when missionaries are sent to the inner city

WOWPD Blotter

9:43 a.m.

A female was reported drinking a cup of cappuccino in a Starbucks. Arriving on the scene, the officer detected garment lines beneath her shirt. Jumping to action, he brought her down before she could dispose of the evidence.

Temple recommend: CONFISCATED

10:23 a.m.

Following an anonymous tip, an officer found an unopened pack of cigarettes in the desk of an agricultural executive. When confronted with the evidence, the man, an elders quorum secretary, swore he used them only to heal the bruises his cows often receive at the hands of unskilled workers. Likely story.

Temple recommend: CONFISCATED

11:45 a.m.

Officer stopped for lunch break. Nice lunch with double-cheese bacon burger, home fries, super-sized Mountain Dew, ice cream, and dark chocolate bar.

PATRIARCHY
Leave no doubt who's presiding.

Seattle Man Has More in Common with Relief Society Sisters

By Terrill W. Cannon

SEATTLE, WA—Niles Liebhardt, a lifetime member of the church, has been struggling in his calling as scoutmaster. "The kids are great," he says, "but I'm not much of a camper, so they just get frustrated with me. Once I sense they're getting restless, then I get frustrated because I can't give them what they want. It's just a vicious circle from that point on."

Liebhardt, a pastry chef, doesn't hunt or fish, and until recently he didn't even own a backpack. "I know it's strange—especially for Seattle—but I'm not really a thrill-seeker," says Liebhardt. "I like to garden and cook, but that doesn't help these fathers train their boys the way they want them trained. It seems like perhaps I'd thrive better in another section of the vineyard."

Often called upon to teach Enrichment lessons for the sisters, Liebhardt has become something of a stake-wide sensation. "You should see him in action," says Alice Baymont, the Greenlake Ward Relief Society president. "He sews, irons, grows his own herbs, and really understands how to work with puff pastry." Baymont confessed that Liebhardt's pie crust makes hers "seem like wallpaper paste." Liebhardt says it's just a matter of keeping all the ingredients chilled and then not overworking the dough. "I also don't use a food processor. It's too violent. Believe it or not, your hands are the best tools once you've cut in the shortening—oh, and be sure to use ice water!"

While Liebhardt is well loved among the sisters, the brethren are less sanguine. "Well, it's kind of strange," says Burt Chamberlain, the Greenlake Ward's physical facilities coordinator. "You can't talk to him about the Seahawks or the Huskies, and I don't think he's ever cleaned a gun. It's kind of like talking to your wife, except, of course, he's wearing a tie."

Liebhardt himself recognizes the tensions, particularly those that arise from the amount of time he spends with the women in the ward. "But there's nothing untoward going on," Liebhardt says. "I'm just trying to get away from all these football-hunting-fishing, overhead-cam-dual-exhaust conversations. When you're with the sisters, you can talk about marzipan and Jane Austen movies and not feel like a fool."

Though he is married with three kids—ages seven, four, and six months—people have questions. Stan Harris, Liebhardt's bishop, thinks something dainty might be going on behind the scenes. "Liebhardt might just find himself thrown out of Scouting at the national level, and maybe that's what he's going for, but it could get a whole lot more complicated real quick for Brother Liebhardt. He wouldn't be able to teach the ladies another word about baklava and hydrangeas unless he got on the dime. That would be a lose/lose situation for everybody."

> **"When you're with the sisters, you can talk about marzipan and Jane Austen movies and not feel like a fool."**

Harris added, "Besides, I haven't been inspired to release him, so I guess he's staying put. Maybe the calling's supposed to teach him a thing or two, firm him up or something. I sure hope so."

Liebhardt isn't threatened by the accusations. He swears allegiance to his wife, saying, "I just happen to like keeping a nice house and cooking wonderful things. If those brethren in the high priest group want to come down to my restaurant and spend a shift busting their humps filling puff pastry with Devonshire cream, they're welcome to it." After a pause, he added, "Those sissies would fold up before eight o'clock."

What will Niles Liebhardt do in the meantime? "Practice lighting campfires," he says, trying his best to look stalwart, "and I guess I'll learn to like canned chili."

Corrections

In our feature article "How to Avoid Home Teaching and Still Achieve Exaltation," we used Elder Jimmy P. Alder as an expert source. It turns out that Alder is not a real general authority and that e-mailing the First Presidency Message is not an effective substitute for home teaching. We regret any convenience this advice may have caused.

In our article about alternative medicine among the Mormons, an editing error led to an inaccurate quote from a spokesman. The incorrect quote stated: "Several church authorities have experienced trepanation, an alternative medicine trend." The correct quote should have read: "Several church authorities have experienced trepidation about alternative medicine trends."

In a recent story, a misprint appeared in our quotation of the hymn "High On a Mountain Top." The correct lyric is "her light shall there attract the gaze," and not, as we printed, "her light shall there attract the gays." We deeply regret any confusion this error may have caused.

Chapter 5:
Comic Relief Society

We Mormon women know we don't have the priesthood, and we know we're only silly little homemakers, and—actually, we're not sure we're really right about this; we'll have to check with the bishop—but, gosh darn it, we *are* still members of the kingdom, second only to our husbands! Sorry, did that sound rude? It probably did, didn't it? Oh my gosh, we are so dumb. We are so sorry.

We'll be sending all of you a chicken casserole and a darling homemade card to apologize. In the meantime, we hope this doesn't sound too forward, and there's no obligation or anything, but you may enjoy reading the following news stories about women in the church. You totally don't have to read them, even. Really. We promise. You can just glance through them if you want—after you've read everything your priesthood leaders have told you to read first, of course. Because that stuff will be much more important.

Okay, sorry to take up so much of your time! We love ya lots!

Area Woman Sacrifices for Her Visiting Teachers

By Kylee-Ashlee Cannon Christiansen

PRICE, UT—The Relief Society visiting teaching program began more than 50 years ago in an effort to help female members learn to love each other and minister to each other's needs. According to local woman Kelly Bolton, the program is a complete success. "By welcoming visiting teachers into my house once a month, I have learned how to be selfless and sacrificing," she confirmed.

After a last-minute call on March 31, Bolton agreed to let her visiting teachers, Sisters Melissa Carter and Joanne Cleaves, come over "for just a quick visit." Bolton, mother of four, then rearranged her schedule to accommodate her visiting teachers. "I don't want to be difficult," she explained. "And I know how much it means to Melissa to get 100 percent on her visiting teaching every year. I couldn't be the one to break her record. She really wants that Lladro statue of Christ that President Thackeray gives every woman who does all her visiting teaching for the year."

Before the 5 p.m. appointment, Bolton cleaned the house, cancelled her son's dental appointment, and asked a neighbor to pick up her daughter from ballet class. "My sister Rachelle called just before the sisters were due to arrive, and she really wanted to talk," said Bolton, "but I just couldn't hang out on the phone and leave them in the living room. That would be inattentive and irresponsible

of me. I have faith that Rachelle will be okay with her postpartum depression until my visiting teachers leave. She'll be taken care of while I'm helping them out."

Despite their promise to be on time and to "just pop in to see how you're doing," Carter and Cleaves were 15 minutes late and stayed for 55 minutes. Their visit included a broad range of conversational topics, including Carter's incredible visiting teaching record, her ambition to become a flight attendant, the amazing place down the road that does Carter's nails for less than anywhere else, the mean lunch lady who obviously hates Carter's daughter Brianne, Cleaves's new cat, Cleaves's son Dakota's swimming trophy, Brother Cleaves's wonderful barbecued ribs recipe, and the Cleaveses' new gorgeous living room carpet and paint.

"I just didn't want to burden them with all my problems. It didn't seem right to use them that way."

"I just didn't want to burden them with all my problems. It didn't seem right to use my visiting teachers that way," said Bolton, explaining why she didn't bring up her sister's depression, her daughter's recent ADHD diagnosis, or her worry that her husband would lose his job in his company's impending layoffs. "Melissa and Joanne love to talk about themselves so much, and I feel it's my duty to create a safe, comfortable environment where they can share their feelings with me."

Bolton wants to tell all the women of the church that the visiting teaching program is inspired. "My visiting teachers have taught me all about service and how to be selfless and giving. I'm more than happy to help Melissa and Joanne grow and progress. Women serving each other—that's what the visiting teaching program is all about."

Misguided Service Project Reflects Unquestioning Love

TWIN FALLS, ID—Anneliese Naylor's quilts may not be as soft and foldable as some, and they may make clanking sounds when you spread them out to cover your child, but "they are just as much an act of love as any of the others," according to Twin Falls Idaho Fifth Ward Relief Society president Sheri Tate.

Naylor's unusual quilts are made of aluminum cans that are bound together and filled with batting. They are a result of what Enrichment leader Marissa Rowntree calls an unfortunate misunderstanding. "When we introduced this Quilts for Kids project, we talked about 'turning aluminum cans into quilts.' I explained that we should all collect cans and recycle them for six months, and use the money to buy fabric and batting." Rowntree added, "I had no idea that anyone would take me so literally. But, bless her, wouldn't you know that Anneliese would."

Naylor says, "I was kind of confused when I heard that we were supposed to make quilts out of cans. I don't have any patterns or any-thing for aluminum-can quilts, and I've never heard of them, but I try to do what I'm told. Maybe aluminum-can quilts are to be used for a higher purpose than we can understand here on earth."

After some fasting and prayer, Naylor set about making empty cans into quilts. She used over five hundred soda cans to make five quilts, sometimes buying cases of soda and pouring it out in order to have enough cans. "Shasta orange cans look really good when you put them next to Barq's cream soda cans," she comments. Her favorite aluminum-can quilt uses Coke cans interspersed with Seven-Up cans, creating a "festive" reindeer pattern. "I just keep seeing a vision of a little child cuddling under my Christmas aluminum quilt," Naylor says. "He looks happy. And he's wearing really soft pajamas so he doesn't bruise."

The unusual quilts took Naylor over four hundred hours to assemble. "I tried sewing a few of the cans together, but after I broke all my needles, I decided to think of something else," she says. "So I found a hole-puncher and tied them together with yarn. It was really hard." However, she says that the hardest part came later: "Oh, definitely the worst part was stuffing batting into all those little holes at the top. They're small and kind of sharp, and I cut up my fingers pretty bad. But I do what my leaders tell me and trust that they know best."

"Maybe aluminum-can quilts are to be used for a higher purpose than we can understand here on earth."

Tate explained that Naylor's misunderstanding isn't a big surprise. "Dear Anneliese doesn't always get it," she says. For example, Naylor didn't understand that the 1997 commemoration of the pioneers arriving in Salt Lake Valley was a reenactment. "She drove all the way down there to 'help the new Saints build their log cabins.' I had to give some stern looks to some of the women who were laughing as she told her story in Relief Society testimony meeting."

While Tate and Rowntree both appreciate Naylor's enthusiasm and acknowledge the hard work she's done, they are concerned about the future of her five aluminum-can quilts. "I took all the other quilts to the local hospital, and they were glad to get them," says Rowntree, "but I don't quite dare bring Anneliese's up there." For now, she says, the quilts lie hidden in her basement under a pile of carpet scraps. "I'm thinking of writing a fake thank-you note from a sick little boy, but I can't tell if that would be kind or cruel."

New Mother Unable to Remember Spelling of Daughter's Name
By Lisa Layton

MESA, AZ—Mary Jane Smith Shumway said that her plain name has been a source of suffering for her entire life. So, to spare her children that suffering, she plans to give them all original, distinctive names. Her first child was recently given a name and a blessing in sacrament meeting, and that name is Shalaynajhezanne Nickoleesa Shumway. Unfortunately, Sister Shumway is often troubled by unforeseen requests to spell her child's name.

"At the doctor's office, or on insurance forms, I am always having to spell it," she said. "It's just so many letters."

Her husband, Nick Shumway, said he predicted problems of this type and worries that teaching Shalaynajezanne to spell her own name will be exceptionally difficult. However, he said, he agreed to the name because "it's kind of pretty."

"Besides," he added, "there are always nicknames. Most of the time I just call her Peanut, because that's what she looked like on the sonogram."

Sister Shumway said that she has learned an important lesson from the experience. "I had the name all picked out: I wanted something unusual for the first name, and for the second, I wanted to name her after her father, Nick. But I hadn't thought about the spelling. Someone at the hospital helped me figure how to spell it on the birth certificate, but I forgot to write it down. Next time, I'll make sure I know how to spell the baby's name before I go to the hospital."

New CTR Ring Miraculously Increases Woman's Spirituality

By Teancum Zenos Smoot IV

SANTA MONICA, CA—Anita Hanks, the new owner of a custom-made, platinum, diamond-encrusted "Choose the Right" ring, has been pleased to note how much her righteousness has increased since its purchase.

"My previous CTR ring was nice," she says, "but the CTR was merely inlaid with 24-karat gold leafing. Ever since I got this upgrade, I've felt a definite increase in spirituality."

The spiritual benefits of the new ring begin in the mornings, when Hanks takes time out of her busy schedule to contemplate the significance of her new ring. "I kneel next to my bed and turn my ring over and over in my hands. I love to count every one of the marquis-cut diamonds that surround the three letters—let's see, I think there are 18 of them—and remember my blessings."

In addition to reminding Hanks of her blessings, the ring also serves as a daily reminder of the covenants she has made. "Every morning, as I lift my ring from the sonic polishing machine and see it glow in all its $80,000 splendor, I remember my own baptism. I wear the ring to help me remember to keep my own soul as pure and shiny."

Since Hanks acquired the ring, her visiting-teaching percentages have skyrocketed, as has her attendance of church activities. "I don't know why it is, but people at church just can't help but comment on my ring," she said.

"I hear that everyone in the ward is talking about it, which makes it hard to be humble. But I've learned a lot of charity by making sure just as many people as possible get to see my ring. And that has been a real blessing in my life because I can tell by the light in people's eyes that they are being inspired to greater righteousness."

The ring also helps Hanks to be righteous when not in church. "When I go out to Nordstrom or to the grocery store, I can tell that people are watching me," said Hanks. "They can tell I'm someone special because I wear my religion on my finger, you might say. So I'm always on my best behavior."

"It's just like the Book of Mormon says: if you are righteous, you shall prosper in the land."

Hanks said she has also noticed an increased sense of compassion toward those less blessed than she is. "Whenever I see a sister who hasn't been blessed, I say a little prayer in my heart for her. Like a sister I saw last week who was wearing a CTR ring that I swear was sterling silver with the normal green paint on the shield. I felt so bad for her, not having the same source of inspiration and righteousness that I have. I would have given her my 18-karat gold CTR ring, but it's the only ring I have that goes with my satin-gold evening gown."

Hanks cites her husband's recent promotion and huge salary increase as one of the many blessings of her increased righteousness. "It's just like the Book of Mormon says: if you are righteous, you shall prosper in the land."

In gratitude, Hanks has commissioned a large CTR to be painted on the bottom of the Hanks family's new Olympic-sized indoor swimming pool.

Vegas Win Attributed to Obeying Law of Tithing

By Lisa Layton

LAS VEGAS—June Brodd of Moline, Illinois, attributed the $1,187 she won after hitting the jackpot on two different slot machines to her faithfulness in paying tithing.

"I've always been a full tithe payer, even when times are tough, and this year, well, they've been really tough," Brodd said. "But heaven has really blessed me for my faithfulness."

Brodd said it was due to inspiration that she ended up going to Vegas in the first place. "My husband Jim works for John Deere, and they were having a convention in Las Vegas. Knowing how sinful it is, there was no way I was going to go with him. But the night before Jim made the travel arrangements, I was channel surfing because nothing was on. I felt inspired to stop on the History Channel, which I never watch. It turned out there was a show about Mormons and Las Vegas."

The show convinced Brodd that it would be all right to visit the Nevada resort town after all. "I learned that Mormons settled Las Vegas in the 1800s to begin with, and that it was a Mormon named Parry Thomas who persuaded Jimmy Hoffa and the Teamsters to finance several of the big casinos. I knew that if a worthy priesthood holder was involved, it had to be OK. Besides, Jim could deduct the entire cost of the trip as a business expense."

After checking into Caesars Palace, Brodd got $25 in tokens for the dollar slots. "Jim and I figured that if I set a limit, it would be OK—it wouldn't really be gambling, it would just be entertainment," she said. But to her surprise, after spending only $18 she hit a jackpot of $741.

"If you pay your tithing, you will find ways to meet your other financial obligations."

"You could have knocked me over," Brodd said. "All this money just came pouring out." Brodd collected her winnings and then moved to another machine. "I still had $7 of my original tokens left," she explained.

Brodd admitted she had to acquire additional tokens before hitting the second jackpot. "I spent $38, and the jackpot was smaller—only $446. Still, altogether it's a nice chunk of money, slightly more than what we need to repair the minivan," Brodd said, tears forming in her eyes. "I just didn't know how we were going to pay for it, and then this windfall came. It really is proof to me that if you pay your tithing, you will find ways to meet your other financial obligations."

Know Your Mormon Terms

Second Combing: When Jesus returns to earth, this time with a church-approved hair style

Relief Society Develops Powder-Puff Self-Defense Class

By Kylee-Ashlee Cannon Christiansen

SPRINGVILLE, UT—In an effort to make the women of the Springville 26th Ward more independent, but "not in a bad, aggressive way," Enrichment leader Connie Weaver has started an ongoing self-defense class "specifically designed for women who don't really want to make anybody upset." Weaver commented that "traditional self-defense classes are way too violent, and we just didn't want to emulate the world."

The class represents a "radical departure" for volunteer teacher Kyra McNeely, a non-member who has a black belt in karate. "I thought I'd teach them some basic self-defense moves for fending off an attacker, such as a fist in the solar plexus or a thumb in the eye," she said. But she admits that she was "unprepared" for the specific needs of the class.

"I just couldn't handle the idea of—of—sticking my thumb in someone's eye," said Michelle Farkas, an attendee who was visibly shaken after the "horrible violence" of the first session. "That's just awful to think of hurting someone like that. That poor man. If I even tried to do that, I'd probably burst into tears." She then burst into tears.

Another attendee of the first session, Erin Spivak, said, "The teacher tried to convince us to carry mace with us wherever we went, but mace is just such a violent thing that it would make me really sad every time I saw it." She added, "Heaven wouldn't want me to hurt anyone." Spivak was "too frightened" to attend the second session.

McNeely said that the first session helped her to "radically reinvent" the content for the class, which will be held on a quarterly basis. "We've talked about how the women don't need to apologize to their attacker for hurting them," she commented. "Next time I'll try to explain that spontaneous hymn-singing really won't stop a rapist."

"We're light-years away from teaching them to knee someone in the groin."

During last week's second session, the attendees sat and listened while McNeely addressed them from behind a podium. "They seem the most comfortable with that format," she commented. Topics of discussion included not smiling at strangers, not letting male hitchhikers into the car just because they might have the priesthood, and not opening the door for salesmen after dark, even if they are selling gospel-oriented products. Though McNeely said that such advice is "pretty obvious," she admitted that her students seemed to need it. However, she added that "sooner or later we'll have to move them beyond just listening to a lecture with soft music in the background to actually trying out some self-defense moves."

According to McNeely, "We're light-years away from teaching them to knee someone in the groin. Maybe I'll just have to teach them how to live happy, fulfilling lives behind their own locked doors."

Relief Society Sister Makes Declarative Statement

By Kylee-Ashlee Cannon Christiansen

HELPER, UT—In a bold move that has sparked discussion and anger in the Helper Second Ward, Sister Rosemary Watts made the following comment in Relief Society last Sunday: "There is absolutely no scriptural evidence to support your theory." The statement was in response to teacher Kathleen Bailey's comment that Bathsheba tempted David by purposefully bathing naked outside his window.

Other Relief Society women said it was the phrasing, not the actual words, that caused the subsequent furor. "Rosemary didn't preface her remark with something like 'Maybe it's just me' or 'I don't know if this is true or not,'" explained Relief Society president Lacey Holding. "She just came right out and said it. Even a milder phrase like 'I was just going to say' would have helped."

Holding's first counselor, Lisa Fowler, says that Watts's comment has "completely ruined" the spirit of peace and friendship among the sisters. "I don't know if this will be a good quote for your story or not, but Relief Society is about love and sisterhood," she says. "Self-effacement is what holds us together. It

makes us feel like no one is smarter than anyone else, so no one feels threatened."

"Maybe I'm wrong, but it seems like authoritative statements are more of a priesthood thing to do."

The Relief Society secretary, Terrie Moore, cites Watts's master's degree in philosophy as the reason for her inability to "get along" with the group. "I guess I'm really stupid compared to Rosemary, but at least I don't make the teacher burst into tears halfway through a class discussion," she said.

"Maybe I'm wrong, but it seems like authoritative statements are more of a priesthood thing to do," said Moore.

F·E·C·U·N·D
for the fertile woman

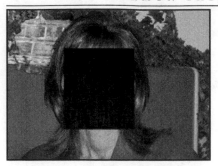

Name Withheld Takes Own Life

DRAPER, UT—After several divorces, an addiction to pornography, sexual abuse, a bout with alcoholism, bankruptcy, not feeling welcome in her ward, homosexuality, multiple spells of church inactivity, and mental illness, Draper resident Name Withheld took her own life Saturday. She was 47.

Withheld wrote many articles about her personal traumas for the *Ensign*, the church's official membership magazine. Among friends, she was known to be anything from manic-depressive to a gambling addict; among *Ensign* readers, she provided hope that they too could "break the cycle."

"I'm always breaking one cycle or another," Withheld said in 1999, just after writing "When a Spouse Has Been Unfaithful" for the *Ensign*. "I worry one day the cycles will start breaking me."

She is preceded in death by several children who also committed suicide, a husband who died, parents who left the church and then died, and a premature baby who died in infancy. She is survived by faithful home teachers who never failed in their duty and a Relief Society president who always kept her in her prayers.

"Sister Withheld was beset by many problems," said her bishop, Randy Taylor. "I'm amazed she didn't do this sooner."

Shirley MacLaine Once Married to Brigham Young
By Molly Thatcher Woodruff

MALIBU, CA—In a recent interview, actress, author, and lecturer Shirley MacLaine revealed that she spent most of her thirty-fourth mortal life as Mrs. Brigham Young in Box Elder County, Utah. In addition, MacLaine announced her intention to write a new biography of the Mormon prophet.

"I detected a gap in my previous life somewhere between the 1850s and 1870s," said MacLaine. "With the help of a past-life channeler, I found out I was one of Brigham's many wives—or 'Briggy,' as I called him in private. So who better than one of the women in his life to tell the real story as it happened?"

MacLaine could not remember much about the Mormon faith, but she said, "I understand they agree with me on a lot of things." Asked if she has read the pivotal biography of Young by late historian Leonard J. Arrington, she said that she has not and was avoiding any previous written material that could taint her memory.

The famous actress is currently trying to contact a few of her reincarnated sister wives.

MacLaine is currently trying to contact a few of her reincarnated sister wives. Additionally, she is working with medium Lola VanDarkegen to contact Arrington about writing the forward to her book. However, Arrington communicated that he was too busy. "It was something about having to catalog and return a collection he'd borrowed from Paradise University," MacLaine said. "But I'm certain everyone will still be pleasantly surprised with the book when it comes out."

Dinner Party Guests Avoid Club Soda

By Lisa Layton

SHOWLOW, AZ—Guests at a recent dinner party hosted by ward singles leader Margaret Cheevers were thrown off guard when Lois Wright, a recently reactivated member, brought a questionable beverage to a dinner party. Not even an opening prayer brought the spirit back into the party after Wright set a bottle of club soda on the table.

"I asked everyone to bring something, and since Lois has been active the shortest, I asked her to bring beverages—you don't ask somebody who's only been coming to church a few months to bring dessert," Cheevers said. "I didn't think it would be a problem."

"I want to avoid even the very appearance of evil, so I wasn't about to have any of that. I'd drink a Coke first."

Wright said that after ten years of bringing a nice merlot to dinner parties she attended, she found selecting beverages for an LDS dinner party very difficult. "I figured the plainer the better, and the grocery store I went to didn't have any flavored seltzers, so I just got club soda and Sprite. But no one would drink the club soda."

Marty James, who has been attending singles activities since his divorce three years ago, commented, "All I knew about club soda was that they have it in bars and you can mix it with alcohol. I want to avoid even the very appearance of evil, so I wasn't about to have any of that. I'd drink a Coke first."

Wright said she is sorry for the confusion and will be more careful about her beverage selections in the future. "But I just didn't think there could be any harm in plain carbonated water, no matter what it gets mixed with."

Cheevers, for her part, said she might be willing to try club soda sometime in the future, now that she knows what it is, "provided my kids aren't around."

Other dinner guests declined to comment.

Mormon Community Awards

Longest home teaching visit (1 hour, 36 minutes): Robert Follett, Provo, UT

Reading every word of the *Ensign* **during 2005:** Marjorie Williams, Malad, ID

Going a whole week without calling the bishop: James Ferguson, Sugar, TX

Inner Child Found, Baptized
By Teancum Zenos Smoot IV

WEST NEWTON, MA—After years of searching, Lola Tolman was pleased to finally come in contact with her inner child last Thursday. "But I found out that she does sinful things, like making fart noises with her armpits and stealing candy from the jar on my kitchen counter," said Tolman. "And ... other things."

In an effort to curb her inner child's behavior, Tolman contacted the missionaries and had her baptized. "Now I need to teach her to hold still and fold her arms during Primary," said Tolman. "My inner child is such a handful."

SNAPSHOT

What are we hiding behind the portrait of Jesus that hangs in our family rooms?

The sword of Laban

Portrait of Pastor Moon

Time portal

Proof that Bush rigged both of his elections

Tunnel out of this hellhole (almost completed)

Safe containing priesthood line of authority

Vaguely pornographic water stain

Views from the Street

Mormonism emphasizes discipline, hard work, and perfectionism. How do you cope with your guilty feelings?

"I don't think I feel enough guilt, and I feel terrible about that."

"I've totally eradicated my guilty feelings by dedicating myself to daily prayer, binge eating, and Zoloft."

"I withhold sex from my husband until he tells me I'm perfect."

"I allow myself 15 minutes of bleak despair and crushing depression each day, while the baby naps."

"I channel my guilt into more constructive outlets, such as criticizing others."

"The same thing I do with all my emotions: shove it way down deep inside and let it fester."

Martha Stewart's Pending Baptism Causes Spike in Utah Antidepressant Use

By Terrill W. Cannon

SALT LAKE CITY—Last week Utah's already high rate of antidepressant use jumped by a factor of six amid reports that the East Coast maven of the domestic arts, Martha Stewart, was taking the LDS missionary discussions and had committed herself to baptism.

Word of the impending baptism spread quickly from ward to ward, as nervous women struggled to imagine how to live their lives with the bar suddenly raised from Sheri Dew to Martha Stewart.

This bittersweet information first reached the Wasatch Front in a weekly e-mail message from Elder Brandon Wolfe, who reported to his parents that he and his companion had been tracting in the Hamptons and found Stewart reeling drunk behind an antique store with a bottle of Dom Perignon in one arm and a cracked orange Fiesta Ware pitcher in the other.

"We told her about repentance and forgiveness, and her whole face lit up," wrote Elder Wolfe. "She was golden, you guys. I've never seen anything like it. It's usually so hard to get these rich people to open up to the gospel, but not Martha. She really wants to change her ways."

Elder Wolfe's mother, Eileen, reported that

her son was gaining weight and developing a taste for coconut chiffon and capers. "I gather that Martha has the elders over to dinner all the time," Sister Wolfe said. "Brandon says she's talking about having them on the show to make funeral potatoes. At least that's what he said when he wrote, asking for the recipe— I could just die. He's going to tell millions of people that this is my recipe, but she'll probably grate those baby red potatoes herself and make her own cream of mushroom soup. I'll never be able to bring that dish to a potluck again. This is not a good thing."

> **"The pressures to keep a wonderful home in Zion have been difficult enough. Having Martha Stewart among us is going to make it impossible."**

Stories like Eileen Wolfe's have become commonplace. Lately the mildest of LDS women can be seen loading bricks of Oasis and rolls of off-white ribbon into their SUVs in order to rework Relief Society centerpieces. Lavelle Viola of Springville, Utah, refused to prepare an Enrichment night dinner, claiming, "If I can't have fresh ahi tuna for the casserole, it's not going to be worth eating." Viola then indicated that "the pressures to keep a wonderful home in Zion have been difficult enough. Having Martha Stewart among us is going to make it impossible. I already feel like giving up."

Dr. Bruce Orhtmann, director of the Wasatch Center for Domestic Mental Health, says that Utah is going to have to brace itself. "I've been over-prescribing antidepressants to Mormon women for years, but I've never seen anything like this before. Good women have been clotting up the emergency rooms, refusing to budge without their SSRIs." Orhtmann said that the situation is like ▶

THE MORMON TABERNACLE ENQUIRER

"that part in Frankenstein where the villagers are swarming the castle with their torches and pitchforks. One of my patients charged into my office while I was in the middle of a session. She was brandishing one of her shoes and screaming that she'd left behind her Zoloft in Nauvoo. It's going to get worse around here before it gets nice."

Stewart's spokesperson refused to comment on the baptism but did mention that the elders had been on the set as Martha's guests. At the request of health officials, KSL in Salt Lake plans to black out that broadcast, claiming, "It's the right thing to do, given the immensity of the situation."

Youth Advisor Calls for Stricter Standards

STANTON, CA—Lisa Horner, Young Women president of the Stanton Eighth Ward, wants a return to stricter dress standards.

"Shirts so tight you can see every curve and ripple, pants so form-fitting there's nothing left to the imagination," Horner said. The final straw for her was watching youth sports in the cultural hall. "All the bouncing and jiggling! They were wearing short shorts and you could peek at those tightly flexed buns every time they went up to spike the volleyball. Those boys need to know what they're doing to females by dressing in this manner."

WOWPD Blotter

1:15 p.m.
Routine screening of coffee aisle at Smith's Food Store.
Two temple recommends: CONFISCATED

2:11 p.m.
Reports of an acrid smell brought officer to a suburban home. At the door, the officer smelled the aroma of marijuana. Found unhealthy elderly female in hospital bed smoking a joint. Also surrounded by syringe needles and various unknown medications. Woman was so addicted that she had rigged a bag on a metal pole that fed unknown substances straight into her veins. Officer confiscated all for evidence, including a strange rubber pan hidden in the bed. It's too bad, because it looks like she'll die soon. See you in the telestial kingdom, lady.
Temple recommend: CONFISCATED

2:29 p.m.
Joined WoWPD chief for daily donut and Dr. Pepper break. Discussed upcoming hunting trip.

Know Your Mormon Terms

Mormen Doctrine: The fundamental belief that no woman can be part of church leadership

Bishopreck: When the bishop's wife leaves him for another woman

Testimoney: When the financial clerk uses anti-counterfeiting techniques to verify that your cash tithing is real

La-woman-ites: The only people who garner even less respect in the scriptures than the Lamanites

Mormon Women Create Style Show

By Kylee-Ashlee Cannon Christiansen

PROVO, UT—Spurred on by the successes of such shows as *What Not to Wear* and *Queer Eye for a Straight Guy*, five LDS women are in preproduction for their own style show. Titled *Righteously Dressed*, the show pits New York high-power fashionistas against homespun Utah Valley fashion sense.

"It's about time someone brought Utah Valley fashion to a high-profile location like New York," says Mistee Nebeker, one of the show's talents. "Mormon fashion is an idea whose time has come. And now it's time to preach that idea to the entire lost gentile world."

How did five Mormon women get a show of their own? "The five of us are in the same ward," explains Mistee. "A year or so ago we had a lesson in Relief Society about multiplying our talents. We realized that our main talent was visiting the mall together and talking about what everyone who walked by

should be wearing. When we discovered that, it was just a short step to getting our own style show on a local TV station run by our friend who's trying to fill time slots."

The pilot episode features the five Mormon friends—Jalyse, Sharon, Patti, Lurlene, and Mistee—accosting strangers walking down Fifth Avenue and offering to make them over. "We met the sweetest young man named Xavier who was dressed in really unfortunate clothing, bless his heart," says Mistee. "He had on these jeans with an unpronounceable French label and a yellow silk shirt, along with some very battered Doc Martens. I mean, that's not an ensemble that sends out a very uplifting message, is it? And I didn't even mention the fringed and battered leather jacket. Heavens."

"She's going to really start sensing her divine potential now that she's covering up those legs."

In the pilot episode, the women and Xavier fly to Orem's University Mall, where they put together a look for him that "just screams 'I'm a nice returned-missionary type of guy!'" says Jalyse. They found him a short-sleeved white shirt, a red medallion tie from Missionary Emporium, some dark brown wing-tips "with some really fun detail stitching," and khaki Dockers from the Gap. "Really, the Dockers are the key item that pulls the ensemble together," says Patti, talking to the other women off-camera while Xavier shows off his new threads on the outside stage at the SCERA shell. "A man just isn't dressed appropriately if he's not wearing khaki Dockers. But now our little city guy looks like bishop material!" ▶

"Plus, the Dockers don't emphasize his—well, what doesn't need to be emphasized, like those tight French jeans do," adds Sharon. "Khaki Dockers are much more modest." All the women agree that the white shirt projects a more mature image, as well. "Maybe this is too worldly of me, but I wonder if he knows that a yellow silk shirt may make some people think that he's G-A-Y," says Lurlene. "But a white shirt and nice red tie? No one will ever think such nasty things about him now!"

The second half of the pilot features a redo of a high-powered African-American magazine editor named Sloane. Again, the women fly Sloane out to the University Mall to "make her look more feminine and more toned down," according to Sharon. They coax her out of her black wool miniskirt and jacket set, her lime-green rayon tank, and her $300 Ferragamo stilettos and find her a cotton floral-print jumper and lace-collar white blouse at Macy's, which Mistee calls "soooo cute, and so feminine, and yet not out of place in the boardroom."

Patti adds, "She can still do her little career girl thing, but now her clothes let men know that she's feminine enough to make a fine wife."

"Plus, the hem is BYU worthy, and you can't go wrong if you adhere to those standards," adds Lurlene. "She's going to really start sensing her divine potential now that she's covering up those legs."

The pilot, which airs in late February, will feature Xavier and Sloane's reac-tions to their new outfits. "Let's just say that not everyone is really ready for Utah Valley style," said Patti. "But that's why we're doing the show—to try to bring all those gentiles out there up to our level."

Predictions for the Future

A manuscript will surface that proves all of Paul H. Dunn's stories true.

Steve Martin will finally own up to his conversion.

New jumpsuit-style uniforms for full-time missionaries will be unveiled.

Two elders serving as missionary companions in Massachusetts will marry.

Book of Mormon moviemaker Gary Rogers will executive-produce *The Proclamation on the Family, The Movie.*

SNAPSHOT

Where are we getting the content for our sacrament meeting talks?

The scriptures: 0.2%

Other church publications: 1.1%

Back of Wheaties box: 7%

Little sister's journal: 16.4%

These damn voices in my head: 17%

The inspirational quotes and faith-promoting urban legends my aunt e-mails me: 58%

Local Woman Fulfills Entire Measure of Her Creation Simultaneously

By M. Spencer Pratt

BOISE, ID—Julia Asner of the Boise 15th Ward is being lauded as an example for all Mormon women everywhere because of her recent achievement. Two weeks ago, Asner announced to family and friends that she and her husband, Jeffrey, are expecting a full complement of six babies. When the sextuplets are born, she will instantly rise to be the head of a large family, thus fulfilling the most noble and perfect goal possible to a faithful woman.

"It is unusual for a woman to be blessed with six miracles at once without the interference of unnatural medical fertility procedures," said Drew Hill, Asner's bishop. "But she swears she did it all on her own, using nothing but good old-fashioned prayer and an all-natural herbal plant estrogen product. So we know that this is truly a blessing from

God, rather than a curse for meddling in God's affairs."

While most women require years, or even decades, to complete their reproductive roles in life, Asner was lucky enough to get it all done early in life. "This is great!" enthused husband Jeffrey. "We've got the whole family coming in one big package. No need to drag it out for year after year after year. I'll need her to hang around for a while and nurture and pass on all her knowledge and whatnot, but what it comes down to is that within a couple of decades, we'll be completely done parenting, and there will be no need for us to hang around any more. We'll be able to pop right back to heaven decades earlier than most people!"

"We've got the whole family coming in one big package."

This kind of efficiency should be encouraged, according to Bishop Hill. "Look, the whole point of this life is to get spirits down here, through their lives, and out the other end," he explained. "The quicker we can get people through, the better. We're trying to figure out a tasteful way to encourage this throughout the ward and, in fact, the entire stake. The biggest problem so far seems to be that people are uncomfortable using the word *sextuplets*."

Julia herself is becoming more comfortable with her position as a role model. "Yeah, I think it will be great," she said. "I mean, I'll probably miss some of my friends at the law firm at first, but I know I'm doing what I was put on this earth to do. And if that means lying on my back in bed for six months, well, then, so be it."

Deseret Book Releases "Pedestal Wife"

By Kylee-Ashlee Cannon Christiansen

SALT LAKE CITY — Deseret Book has announced a new product that can "help Mormons bring the Spirit into the home." Called Pedestal Wife, the new product resembles a statue of a woman who's five feet, six inches tall, with short, curly brown hair, a sensible dress, and an apron, standing on a marble pedestal two feet high. Deseret Book stresses, "Pedestal Wife is more than just a statue, although she does certainly beautify and brighten the home. She is primarily designed to help us all glorify womanhood."

One of the first consumers, Provo resident Aaron L. Nabaum, reports that he is pleased with Pedestal Wife. "I installed her in the living room so the family can gaze lovingly on her while we do our daily scripture reading," he says. "It's so nice to have her there for those times during family home evening when we talk about women's holy nature and how much less sinful than men they are. Plus, she's a lot easier to get along with than my own wife, bless her heart."

Although response to the product has been mostly positive, Orem native Justin Peterson admits he was initially confused by Pedestal Wife's purpose. "I put her in my kitchen, hoping she would make me some of those incredible apple dumplings my mom used to bake on winter afternoons," he admits. "I didn't realize she'd just stand there. Eventually, we moved her to the bedroom, and while my wife isn't happy with that, I am."

Peterson's experience is not unusual. The confusion about Pedestal Wife's role prompted the release of an official statement from Deseret Book: "While Pedestal Wife does encourage the healthy glorification of womanhood and thereby increases spirituality, consumers need to remember that the product is not actually designed to interact with them in any meaningful way. She does not talk, cook, or form relationships."

Despite these and similar misunderstandings, however, Pedestal Wife is selling very well and has gained a loyal following, mostly of married men who live along Utah's Wasatch Front. "I don't know what it is—that apron, the dress, or the twenty-four-inch waist—but somehow Pedestal Wife reminds me of my saintly mother," says Ogden resident Aaron McClellan. "That woman raised eight children in a three-room house, had a hot meal on the table three times a day, and managed to read the Book of Mormon over a hundred times." McClellan's wife Meredith was not available for comment.

Know Your Mormon Terms

Kolube: Even in heaven, you have to change your oil every 3,000 miles

Priest-in-the-hood: What was made available in 1978 to every worthy African-American male

Centerpiece Correlation Committee Founded

By Kylee-Ashlee Cannon Christiansen

SALT LAKE CITY—In reaction to "great concern" expressed by the general Relief Society board, the church has established a new committee to regulate the centerpieces used in Relief Society lessons and "ensure that these centerpieces bring women closer to God," according to Elder Milton P. Lamoreaux.

Sister Beverly R. Grumman, second counselor in the general Relief Society presidency, said, "Relief Society centerpieces are crucial to the success of women's education in the church. Because of their importance, it is high time that these items fell within the jurisdiction of a priesthood-supervised committee." She noted that too many women are creating "frivolous" centerpieces for their lessons and not adequately considering the effect of these items on the women in the class.

President Sharon Oakes agrees that the committee is a "dire necessity." She has visited too many wards where Relief Society centerpiece creation has caused tension and

despair, rather than a feeling of sisterhood. "Many sisters display inappropriate items and colors, such as bright-purple silk irises or non-church-approved family photographs," she says. "Not all sisters understand that their fake flowers should be pastel or pale colors, so as not to detract from the lesson. And carnations, for example, are much more decorous than irises."

Failure to grasp the difference between appropriate and inappropriate centerpiece items is not the only problem the Relief Society presidency notices. Many other sisters feel "simply inadequate" when faced with overly elaborate centerpieces in their Relief Society room, according to Sister Grumman. "These sisters should see Relief Society as a haven from the world. Instead, if they are faced with a perfectly arranged two-foot bouquet of silk flowers and three Lladro statues of Christ, many of them experience self-esteem problems."

"Friendships are ending, and animosities are building. Thank heavens the priesthood has stepped in to help."

The sisters of the Bonneville West Stake in Layton, Utah, are "relieved" that their centerpiece decisions will now be overseen by an official priesthood body. "Our centerpiece situation has been just awful this past year," claims Denise Raymond, a twenty-five-year-old homemaker. "I mean, like, the women always work like crazy on them and spend tons of money. And that harms our self-esteem."

Sister Raymond recalls a time last ▶

summer when her friend, Lara Beatton, spent twenty hours creating an elaborate three-foot-tall replica of the Salt Lake Temple out of toothpicks for her lesson on temples. "Ten women walked in that day and saw it and burst into tears," she said. "They wouldn't speak to Lara for months. Two of them had to go on Paxil. And I totally understand. How does she expect us to compete with that? How can we feel we're real women with something like that testifying to our inadequacy? How can anyone feel happy in Relief Society anymore? We so obviously need the priesthood to help us with our centerpiece problems."

Sixty-seven-year-old Edna Gambel agrees. "These young girls don't understand how to make appropriate centerpieces these days," she said. "You wouldn't believe the shockingly unspiritual things I've seen. They've abandoned crewelwork for cross-stitched samplers. They don't macramé anymore. And I haven't seen a lovely frosted-glass grape since I don't know how long. Instead, all I see these days are those distressed and painted boards with cute sayings on them. Did I mention those boards are distressed? What's wrong with Precious Moments figurines, after all?"

Sister Gambel's remarks underscore the danger of keeping centerpiece decisions uncorrelated, according to President Oakes. "The situation is so chaotic that these women don't even know what's appropriate anymore. Friendships are ending, and animosities are building. Thank heavens the priesthood has stepped in to help."

Prediction for the Future

Some reality TV show will have a Mormon on it, and everyone will spend hours debating whether he or she reflected well or poorly on the church.

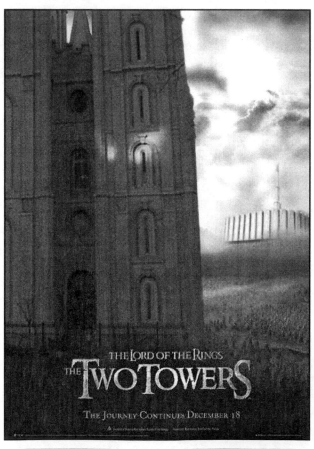

Zions Bank Offers Financing for Scrapbookers

By Milton P. Romney

OREM, UT—The State Street branch of Zions Bank has announced special financing for scrapbook projects that otherwise might be beyond some people's budgets. Loan officer Linda Cowling explains that while Zions does not promote the accumulation of unnecessary debt, "there are just some times when you need help with that particularly important page. That's where we come in." Response to the program has been "brisk," she said.

"We've been counseled to avoid debt for things besides a house and our education," says Enrichment board member Wendy Burgenhoffer of the American Fork 89th Ward. "But keeping a scrapbook is virtually a commandment, isn't it? I mean, judging from the women in my ward, I'd say it's right up there with the Word of Wisdom. I'm not even sure I could get a temple recommend if I didn't magnify my collection of stamps, border scissors, and gel pens. I've got a closet full of scrapbooks, but last week my husband sprung it on me that I'll have to do more than teach piano on Tuesdays if I want to keep this

up, because he's on the verge of declaring bankruptcy. However, I'm not going to work outside the home just to pay his bills, so a loan makes perfect sense to me."

Other scrapbookers in the area agree that this opportunity for special financing is timely. Lindsay Owendorf of the Orem Hilltop Ward said, "I've had single pages that cost me well over $1,000, and that's not the kind of thing we planned for when I committed to attend Enrichment night years ago. I had this one page commemorating our family trip to Nauvoo that, in my mind, simply had to be made of authentic Egyptian papyrus from the tomb of Amenhotep IV. And you don't just put little stamps and stickers on a page like that." Owendorf said she hired a local calligrapher to use gold ink to handprint the captions under the photos in a style reminiscent of true Egyptian hieroglyphics. "My husband wept when he saw that page," she recalled. "I assume it was the Spirit that moved him and not so much the Visa bill."

> **"My husband says I'll have to do more than teach piano on Tuesdays if I want to keep scrapbooking, because he's on the verge of declaring bankruptcy."**

Luella Romrell of the Springville Edgemont Ward admits that she's been known to spend a month's worth of her family's grocery budget on a single scrapbook project. "I just knew the Lord would bless us for my faithfulness in this all-important area of the ▶

kingdom, and he did! We managed to live off ramen noodles and Kool-Aid for three weeks before Luke got his next paycheck." She notes with some bitterness, however, that in spite of her sacrifices Luke left her and their eight children for a "floozy who's never darkened the door of Relief Society her whole life." Romrell believes this never would have happened had scrapbook financing been available in her hour of need.

Local church leaders are encouraging their ward members to take advantage of the low financing rates in meeting their scrapbooking obligations. Gerald S. Moore, bishop of the Provo 277th Ward, indicates that several members of his flock have fallen behind on their tithing due to scrapbook-related expenses. "With the benefits of this loan program, our members can once again keep all the commandments, including their obligation to appropriately commemorate every trip, ball game, school performance, and birthday party their children ever have," he says.

Terms of the loan range from 12 months to 30 years, depending on the size of the project. Authorization requires written approval from the applicant's husband and bishop.

Predictions for the Future

All of Europe will be consolidated into one mission staffed by 25 missionaries.

Hubble Space Telescope scientists will positively identify Outer Darkness and make progress in their search for Kolob.

Corrections

Last month, we erroneously stated that serving as ward financial clerk requires more revelation than serving as ward Relief Society president. In addition, we neglected to mention that the Relief Society president we interviewed is a jujitsu expert. We regret the error more than you can possibly imagine.

In a profile of Bishop Trevor Wilkinson, who has achieved the church's highest rate of successful marriage counseling, we mistakenly reported that he keeps a copy of *The Joy of Sex* on his office bookshelf. In reality, the book is *The Joy of Tex-Mex*.

Anybody want some wheat? That's more of a question than a correction, but we do have plenty in our food storage, if you need any.

And when the children of Israel saw it, they said one to another, It is manna: for they wist not what it was.
Exodus 16:14-15 Reach for **Manna**

Chapter 6:
Programs and Policies and Procedures–Oh My!

At some point, Mormonism went from being less about prophets and peepstones and priesthood and more about programs and policies and procedures. During the twentieth century, the church evolved into a modern corporation that sometimes seems to fit more naturally into the Fortune 500 than into—well, if there isn't a Spiritual 500 list, someone ought to start maintaining one.

Usually it's pretty easy to predict where the church corporation will go next. Occasionally, however, it zigs when you expect it to zag—and that's when *The Mormon Tabernacle Enquirer* swoops in to report the facts. Whether at the grassroots stake level or churchwide, policies, programs, and procedures are constantly evolving, and you can count on us to help you keep tabs on this dynamic organization.

of Cougar Stadium. "This is indeed a great day for the church," said L. Mack Quinn, elders quorum president of the Provo 1,001st Ward. "Long will the members of this church remember this wonderful event. Parents will tell their children—and they'll tell their children—of the first temple launching."

"It was quite a task getting the Provo Temple into the air," admitted the launching team's senior engineer.

"This reminds me of that great prophesy in Jeremiah," said Sally Thompson, Spanish Fork Spring Heights Ward Primary song leader. "And behold, I looked up, and beheld a flying roll." Indeed, the Provo Temple, as it spun toward the ionosphere, resembled many things. Some described it as a ball of fire. Others said the temple looked like the Angel Moroni standing on top of a huge steeple of smoke.

Provo Temple Liftoff Successful
By Teancum Zenos Smoot IV

PROVO, UT—Smoke billowed around the base of the Provo Temple Thursday morning as its thrusters fired, sending the structure rocketing into the sky. People watching from the surrounding area cheered, waved their neckties, and hugged one another as the structure sailed past the giant Y emblazoned on the mountain.

Lucky LDS missionaries had a prime view from the Missionary Training Center. "The church is true, the church is true," Elder Marshall Cleo repeated to himself, tears streaming down his face as he watched the liftoff from the complex's front lawn. Cleo had come to the MTC only one week earlier to prepare for a mission in Pennsylvania.

Local leaders and media personnel watched the launching from the fish bowl

From the nosebleed section of the BYU stadium, freshman Robbie Bennett commented, "Man, that is one crazy pre-game show."

The Provo Temple liftoff is the inaugural event in the church's temple-launching program, which is being funded by special donations from members. "It was quite a task getting the Provo Temple into the air," admitted Joe P. Costello, senior engineer of the launching team. "Things had to be checked over and over again to make sure nothing went wrong during the crucial moments."

The church has issued a statement that it will erect a monument to the successful launch on the site where the temple formerly stood. The possibilities of attempting a twin-booster launch of the Logan Temple and a six-booster launch of the Salt Lake Temple were also announced.

Mysterious Device Discovered in Meetinghouse

By Kylee-Ashlee Cannon Christiansen

MAGNA, UT—As of last Sunday, the roof of the Magna West Stake Center supports a large, metal device that was previously hidden. No one seems to know what it is or how it got there.

The church's only issued statement does not discuss the nature of the device. "We regret to announce that the Magna West Stake Center is closed, effective immediately, until further notice," announced a spokesman. "No one is allowed in the building or within a quarter mile of the premises. In fact, we highly recommend you don't look up there or even think too much about it. Just carry on with your daily business."

Although no official word has been given, local members have come to a general consensus about the nature of the device.

"Holy mackerel, that is one heck of a doozy of a gun up there," said Brother Dwayne Strull, a retired rancher. "They weren't kidding about that whole 'Onward Christian Soldiers' hymn and all that war talk in the Book of Mormon. I don't want to be on the wrong side of the Mormons now, sure as you're born."

Other ward members agree that the device is an armament of some kind. "Dude, it looks exactly like that Extreme Peace-Making ZX2000 Flame-Thrower you can get on that one secret level of Doom," said Marcus Smoot, a deacon. "This is flat-out the awesomest thing I've ever seen at church." Smoot was then unexpectedly escorted off the premises by three security officials wearing dark suits and sunglasses.

It has been rumored that the unexpected addition to the church building was discovered when Wayne Johnston and Anthony Diamond, both sixteen, found a hidden staircase that led up to an attic where the unnamed device was stored. Diamond's friend, Rob Bowden, claims the device had an active timer attached, which was counting down to an unspecified date approximately three years away. Johnston and Diamond are currently in custody and were unable to issue a statement.

"I don't want to be on the wrong side of the Mormons now."

Church representatives will not say how the device was discovered or reveal what it is. At the press conference, Riggle waved his hand and claimed, "There was no cannon discovered." When asked if he had just actually attempted to perform the Jedi mind trick on the reporters, a visibly flustered Riggle announced that the press conference was over.

Mormon Community Awards

Briefest closing prayer when the meeting ran overtime (11 words): Kip Rollins, Mesa, AZ

Best funeral potatoes: Lindsay Lombino, Cherry Hill, NJ

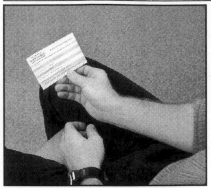

Numbering System Created for Sunday School Answers
By LeVoy Mann

RIVERTON, UT—Stakes in the Riverton area have implemented a new numbering system to help streamline Sunday school lessons for members. "The new system was made not only to alleviate problems with the reliability of answers given by class participants," said spokesman Richard Nibley, "but also to create a speedier, more efficient learning process."

Class members will now be expected to say a number in answer to a question instead of putting their thoughts into words. The new system is shown below.

The number system was devised to address concerns with off-topic and too-detailed answers offered by some classroom participants. "There are also those who are answering more often than three times a lesson and tying up teachers' time with lengthy stories, speculations, and interpretations," explained Nibley.

"I can feel inspiration much more strongly when I don't have to think so hard about the answers."

"I've already seen a big difference," said Elayhne Robinson of the Riverton Fourth Ward. "I can feel inspiration much more strongly when I don't have to think so hard about the answers. Besides, what do I care about other people's experience and insights into the doctrine?"

The stakes are allowing the continued use of hand-raising instead of a proposed buzzer system. In wards where "serious question-answering problems exist," the new policy will be strictly enforced by a uniformed official sitting at the back of the class and armed with a foam rubber baton.

THE CHURCH OF
JESUS CHRIST
OF LATTER-DAY SAINTS
Answer Numbering Guide

1 = Prayer

2 = Fasting

3 = Reading the scriptures

4 = Paying your tithing

5 = Obeying the Word of Wisdom

6 = Through some experience in my lifetime,
I have received a personal testimony of this principle.

Remember to raise hand and speak the number clearly.   © LDS Sunday School Services

---

Deseret Book Now an "Opposition-Free Zone"

By Teancum Zenos Smoot IV

SALT LAKE CITY—To complement Deseret Book's policy of not stocking books with "excessive profanity, heavy violence, and immorality," the LDS retail chain has launched a marketing campaign celebrating its bookstores as an "opposition-free zone."

"We are pleased to offer a celestial environment where the righteous decisions have already been made for the customer," said spokesperson Mark Stringham during a press conference announcing the new campaign.

"Before this policy, there was always the chance that our customers might buy a book that would seriously deal with sin and its effects," said Stringham, his eyes tearing up. "Through a survey, we found that our customers expect that a church-owned bookstore should not only refrain from promoting sin but from even talking about it."

Bonnie Smithers, standing in the *Work and the Glory* section of Deseret Book that now takes up half the store, where the classics, science fiction, fantasy, and humor sections used to stand, wept with gratitude when she heard of the new policy.

"I feel so safe here now," she said. "I know that now I won't even have the choice of buying something that might portray sin. I remember seeing a copy of *1984* here once, and I felt inspiration leave me immediately. I just know I shouldn't be reading books like that."

A press release claims that customers can expect to see a twenty to thirty percent increase in their spirituality just by entering the store. "Increasing your testimony has never been easier," the press release reads.

"I don't know why we didn't think of it before," Stringham continued. "The less opposition there is, the more growth can occur and the more money we can earn."

As part of the retailer's new emphasis, it will no longer carry the Old Testament, because of the story about Lot impregnating his two daughters; the New Testament, because an adulteress appears in it; the Book of Mormon, because of the gratuitous violence Ammon inflicted when chopping off the arms of Lamanites; and the Doctrine and Covenants, because it contains an entire section condoning plural marriage, an excommunicable offense today.

"And definitely not the Pearl of Great Price," Stringham added. "It has naked people running around outdoors in a garden."

Church Warns Against Cola-Flavored Sprite

By Jack B. Kimball

ATLANTA, GA—Just days after the introduction of a cola-flavored version of Sprite, the church issued a warning about the new product. "We see this as an insidious corruption of something pure and acceptable to Latter-day Saints," said spokesman Carl Spainhower. "This is a gateway drink to harder soda, as potentially dangerous as so-called nonalcoholic beer."

Although Spainhower acknowledged that cola-flavored Sprite could help adults wean themselves from an addiction to real cola, he warned that using the drink in public might represent a failure to avoid the appearance of evil. "We continue to encourage members to opt for caffeine-free colas," Spainhower said. "The distinctive caffeine-free packaging sends a clear message of righteousness."

Arnold Friberg Body-Building Program Announced

By Teancum Zenos Smoot IV

SALT LAKE CITY—A new addition to the Word of Wisdom has been announced that will help "strengthen the membership," according to spokesperson Michael Valdez. This new addition is being called the Arnold Friberg Exercise Program.

"Arnold Friberg's famous paintings of the muscular Ammon and Nephi are not mere metaphors for spiritual strength, as some misguided people will tell you," said Valdez. "They are a standard that every member should live up to."

Valdez said that all members will soon be held accountable for the new program. Body-fat estimation, cardiovascular fitness, and bicep measurement will become a regular part of temple recommend interviews within the year. "One of the upshots of this new revelation," said Valdez, "is that the gospel will be more attractive to potential converts, because our members will be more attractive than they are now."

The Friberg program started in secret a few years ago with a pilot program that trained senior couple missionaries in daily aerobic exercise and weight training. "Since Abinadi looks that good, they were willing to give it a shot," said Valdez. So far, the results have been quite successful.

"I want to get as close to my perfect resurrected body as I can in this life."

"I'm starting to feel like my newfound strength allows me to share the gospel more effectively," said Elder Thor G. Krogstad, who now bench-presses 300 pounds. "Whenever I find myself in an antagonistic situation while preaching, like if someone is threatening me or shouting anti-Mormon doctrine, it really

changes the whole tone of the situation when I flex and split the back of my suit coat. My wife likes it too."

In addition, the Friberg program has been greeted with enthusiasm by young male LDS missionaries all over the world. Elder Todd Healy of the Florida Tallahassee Mission said, as he worked on his thirtieth set of military presses, "I figure I want to get as close to my perfect resurrected body as I can in this life."

Rank-and-file members are also excited about the Friberg program. "The effects of the program will certainly help me when I imagine my congregation in their underwear," said Bishop Andrew Richards, who often uses that tactic to relieve his pulpit anxiety.

Views from the Street

What are your favorite general conference traditions?

"Falling asleep on the couch, which is much more comfortable than falling asleep on the stand."

"I like to count how many times they zoom in on the black choir member."

Church Leaders Perform Mass Food Blessing

By M. Spencer Pratt

SALT LAKE CITY—In a meeting led by Elder Alan D. Quinlisk at an undisclosed location, a blessing was pronounced on "all food eaten anywhere, by anyone, at any time present or future." What has already become known as the MegaBlessing is expected to save thousands of man-hours each year because members will no longer have to bless each meal individually.

A jubilant Elder Quinlisk announced the action in a press conference. "Well, we did it. We weren't sure we'd have enough faith to bring it off, but we pulled together and did it! Woo! Afterwards, we were all high-fiving and hugging each other, we were so excited. Wow. What a moment!"

Although the exact wording of the prayer has not yet been released, Quinlisk assured reporters that the combined agricultural and livestock output of the world has now been blessed with the ability to "nourish and strengthen our bodies" and will now "do us the good we need" in perpetuity. In addition, the blessing extends to all the "hands that prepared it."

"It was originally Gene's idea," said Quinlisk, referring to Elder Eugene L.

D'Avolio. "When he was a mission president, he once blessed all the food in all his missionaries' apartments so they'd have more time to proselyte. When he was called to a higher position, he figured, hey, why not?"

Church members have received the news joyfully. "What an inspired idea!" said Taylorsville member Susan Kendall. "I'm so tired in the morning that sometimes I fall asleep while blessing my breakfast. And whenever I let the kids bless dinner, it would be cold by the time they were done and no one could understand what they said anyway. Now all that is a thing of the past!"

The combined agricultural and livestock output of the world has now been blessed with the ability to "nourish and strengthen our bodies."

The MegaBlessing is not all encompassing, however. Quinlisk pointed out that "substances prohibited by the Word of Wisdom will continue to be cursed."

The success of the MegaBlessing has prompted speculation about possible follow-ups. "We're considering a MegaBlessing II to bless all travelers in the world that they will arrive home in safety," said Quinlisk. "But that's obviously a much bigger challenge."

Predictions for the Future

A new program to build even smaller temples will be announced. "Think Winnebago," hinted a church spokesman.

Automatic tithing payroll deductions will become available.

"An important part of my spiritual life is opening up my inbox every afternoon and reading the inspirational stories forwarded to me from the sisters in my ward," says Tammi Parker of Orem, Utah, one of the first to be disciplined by local authorities under the new Declaring Unauthorized Miracles (DUM) rules. Parker is accused by her bishop of posting a message to ldsmom.org in which she describes as a "miracle" the very rapid passing of a dime through the intestinal system of her toddler after a priesthood blessing.

Church Tightens Miracle Standards

By Milton P. Romney

"We encourage our members to tell faith-promoting stories. We just want them to tell the ones we have authorized."

SALT LAKE CITY—Responding to a spate of faith-promoting Internet postings by Church members describing miraculous healings, remarkable promptings, angelic visitations, and unanticipated insurance refunds just when they ran out of money, the LDS Church has issued tighter standards regarding the pronouncement of miracles.

"We can ill afford to become as the Catholics," says Church spokesman T. Kimball Ridge, "who will believe that a soap film slightly resembling the Madonna on the window of an adult video store is a sign from the Almighty."

According to the announcement, members are not to declare anything a miracle "until it has been approved by the proper authority." Member reaction to the announcement is mixed. While some are relieved that the pressure is off to recount miraculous events at fast and testimony meeting, others, particularly Internet-savvy stay-at-home mothers, are very disappointed.

"The new rules on this type of thing are clear," says Parker's bishop in the Orem 179th Ward. "Had she brought me the diaper and asked me to seek miracle approval with the Brethren, then we might have gotten her the miracle status she was seeking. But she didn't. She just launched off on her own and determined to speak for the Brethren in this matter, and for that she is being disciplined."

Elder Ridge said, "We continue to encourage our members to tell faith-promoting stories. We just want them to tell the ones we have authorized."

A new family resource book, *Best-Loved Miracles of the LDS People*, is slated for publication early next year. "Members will find all the Church-correlated miraculous accounts they could ever hope to tell in that book," says Ridge. "And they can share them with complete confidence, knowing they have been approved by the proper authorities."

Minions Destroy Member Home
By Milton P. Romney

baby's room don't count for nothin'." Jarvis countered, "Next thing I know, you'll say I gotta pay Greg Olson to paint a life-size portrait of the First Presidency on my garage door."

The stake presidency urges families to hang a Del Parson Savior portrait in a spot that can be seen through the front window of the house.

RIGBY, ID—Nobody was more surprised than Amber Jarvis when Lucifer's minions appeared at her doorstep and proceeded to destroy her home. According to witnesses, the house at 374 North 600 East was leveled within minutes.

"I had just sent the kids off to school and was still in my bathrobe," sobbed Amber Jarvis, a member of the Rigby 39th Ward. "I tried to shoo the minions away, but they just rushed past me and destroyed everything. They are evil, I tell you, just plain evil!"

The Jarvis home is the second in eight months to come to this end. During an interview at the scene, stake president L. Rob Muldoon stated that he specifically warned against this kind of tragedy in last month's stake conference.

"This is a real problem in our stake," Muldoon said. "People have got to understand that homes that fail to prominently display a picture of a temple, a portrait of the Savior, and a copy of the proclamation on the family are little more than hell on earth. And if they'll spend the extra money for huge baroque frames with gold leaf, so much the better."

Ron Jarvis claims that the family did, in fact, have a proclamation hanging in the home. However, President Muldoon said, "Stuff thumb-tacked to the wall in the

Beehive Bookstores report a recent run on their temple photos and Jesus portraits, and all home teachers in the Rigby Stake are delivering a new copy of the proclamation to their families. "We don't want this to happen again," says Muldoon, "at least not to any of our members. What the minions do to the gentiles is not our concern."

In reply, a representative of the minions stated, "The gentiles are not our concern."

Views from the Street

What are your favorite general conference traditions?

"I put on my best Laura Ashley dress, play my Michael McLean CD quietly in the background, bake some bread, and take notes on scented stationery with my butterfly pen."

"Sleeping until noon on Sunday, going to a movie, claiming I'll read the talks in the *Ensign*, then blowing it off."

Mormon Lobbyists Ask Legislature to Drop Seagull as State Bird

By R. Williams

SALT LAKE CITY—The California Gull (*Larus californicus*) is honored by Utah as its official state bird. As Utah schoolchildren learn, when early Utah settlers faced starvation due to hordes of crickets devouring crops, thousands of gulls miraculously appeared and spared some of the crops by eating the insects.

What these children don't learn, and what concerns a group of Mormon lobbyists, is that some gulls form lesbian care-giving relationships. "We are deeply disturbed," wrote group spokesman Don Chapman in a letter to the Utah legislature, "that by honoring this gull we may call attention to its female-to-female bonding and highlight the fact that such relationships exist naturally in the animal kingdom."

The group first learned of the gulls' alternative lifestyles from a BYU family science professor who read a summary of an article from the ornithology journal *Auk*. The article reported that one to two percent of California Gull nests and ten percent of Western Gull nests were cared for by pairs of females, who were able to care for five to six eggs in each nest, versus the normal two to three eggs in traditional male/female nests.

The ultra-conservative Eagle Forum political organization has joined forces with the group on this issue. Mike Conover of the legislature's public affairs office reports that the senate mailroom has received three identical letters from Eagle Forum members urging that the California Gull be replaced with the dodo bird. The letters argue that because the dodo is extinct, no one could prove that it naturally practiced any alternative lifestyles. "My own deepest, most closely held, and most personal fear," read each letter, "is that if Utahns are forced to accept the reality of the seagulls' alternative lifestyles, the next thing you know, the FCC will allow radio and TV to play music composed by so-called gay persons."

"Only traditional families can be legally recognized, because only traditional families are traditional."

When state senator Kay Bryson (R-Kaysville), leader of the legislature's four-member coalition of moderate Republicans, publicly questioned whether the state bird could have any effect on public attitudes toward gender and marriage, Chapman responded with a heated letter to the editor of the *Salt Lake Tribune*. "If Utah retains the seagull as its state bird," he wrote, "people may wonder if it is natural for some humans to form different family units. If our citizens consider this, they may slither down that slippery slope of questioning the whole concept of 'traditional.' Only traditional families can be legally recognized, because only traditional families are traditional."

The Utah legislature has not yet taken any action in response to the lobbying, but Senator Bryson has intimated that the Senate is not likely to bow to the pressure. "If we bow to this silly lobbying, what's next?" Bryson said. "Are we going to have to change the state emblem? After all, just think of the public policy issues implicated by the social structure of the polyandrous beehive."

All-Seeing Eye Proposed for Church Office Building

By Jack B. Kimball

SALT LAKE CITY—Last Thursday, a consortium of scientists and inventors held a press conference to demonstrate the prototype of an "all-seeing eye" they propose to install atop the LDS Church's 28-story office tower in downtown Salt Lake City.

"Through a new spiritual technology we've created, this eye is able to spot disturbances in spiritual well-being up to 100 miles away," said Matthew Kroft, the project's head scientist. "With the eye installed on the Church Office Building, the church will be able to monitor people up and down the Wasatch Front, from Brigham City to Nephi. The eye can see through walls, but mountains are too thick, so we will install ocular relay stations at key points."

With its glowing blue iris suspended between risers on top of the church tower, the 20-foot-diameter eye will be visible throughout the Salt Lake Valley. Constantly revolving, it will emit a searchlight beam at night.

"This eye will be a beacon of light to inspire everyone—including nonmembers—to live more spiritually correct lives," says Kroft.

According to the proposal, whenever the eye detects a significant drop in spirituality in a particular person, a warning letter will be automatically generated to the bishop responsible for the geographical area in which the person's home address is located. "Whether the person is a Mormon or not, the local bishop will invite him in for an interview," says Kroft. "With love and compassion, the bishop will try to find out why the person's spirituality dropped and recommend ways to restore it. Of course, the person has the free agency to decide whether or not to repent."

"This eye will be a beacon of light to inspire everyone—including nonmembers—to live more spiritually correct lives."

In addition to pinpointing individual spirituality, the eye will be able to generate composite spirituality reports for specified areas. "The church can find out what the spirituality index is for, say, Bountiful on a week-to-week basis. If they notice a negative trend, they can start holding emergency firesides without delay."

When the *Enquirer* asked if this idea was inspired by the *Lord of the Rings* movies, Kroft responded, "The only Lord of the rings we know is the one who brought the Olympics to Utah. Look, *somebody* is watching all those QuickTime porn movies at work. We just want to give bishops a better way to look into the hearts of their flock."

At press time, Kroft and his team were still trying to get an appointment with the LDS Church's Strengthening Members Committee.

THE CHURCH OF
JESUS CHRIST
OF LATTER-DAY CHRISTIANS

Petitioners Want "Christian" Added to LDS Church Name
By Jack B. Kimball

SALT LAKE CITY—Citing decades of misunderstanding and downright abuse, the Association for Mormon Christianity announced this morning that more than 20,000 people have signed a petition to officially change the LDS Church's name to "The Church of Jesus Christ of Latter-day Christians," with a corresponding change in acronym to LDC.

"When it comes right down to it, we're actually the only religion with the true right to use the term *Christian*," said association spokesman Steve Eggett. "All the other religions that call themselves Christian are, in fact, abominations. It would be more accurate to refer to themselves as antichrists."

> ## "All the other religions that call themselves Christian are, in fact, abominations."

Asked about the Doctrine & Covenant scripture that states, "For thus shall my church be called in the last days, even The Church of Jesus Christ of Latter-day Saints," (115:3), Eggett said, "In our opinion, this name change is a medium-level correction that should not require a revelatory statement on a par with the priesthood revelation. It's a timely correction, like those textual updates that make the Book of Mormon sound less racist. Anyway, the term *Saints* has always felt awkward, because it sounds self-

aggrandizing and too Catholic."

Religious commentator David Welch said, "It's about time the church took decisive action to once and for all resolve the dispute about whether Mormons are Christian or not. I've long considered this a more pressing issue for the church than issuing an apology for its historic racism toward blacks. On the other hand, I worry this name change could result in less persecution, and the church might start getting cocky."

Spokesman Eggett concluded, "Another side benefit of changing our acronym to LDC is that we will no longer be confused with the perfidious drug LSD. We have grown weary of little jokes transposing the last two letters of our former acronym to imply that we are a hallucinatory people."

Polynesian Dancers to Wear Navel Pasties
By Milton P. Romney

LAIE, HI—Richard L. Hermiston, spokesman for the LDS Church's Polynesian Cultural Center, announced today that all female dancers be required to wear flesh-toned pasties to cover their exposed navels.

Supporters of this latest move to improve modesty at the center are pleased. "It's bad enough the way they wiggle and shimmy their breasts and hips," said one woman, "but seeing their exposed bellybuttons just crossed the line."

In a separate announcement, it was revealed that photos in published materials would be touched up to hide the fact that all the Samoans have "ghastly" tattoos.

Predictions for the Future

The Book of Mormon will be translated into both Klingon and Elvish.

Committee Formed to Honor Pioneers of 1997
By Jack B. Kimball

SALT LAKE CITY—Several years after modern pioneers accomplished a heroic reenactment of the original wagon trek from Nauvoo to Salt Lake City, a committee has been formed to honor and perpetuate their memory.

"It's high time we recognize their bravery and their sacrifice of comforts and precious vacation time," said Gordon Mitchell, president of the new Days of '97 Committee. "These pioneers opened our hearts to our ancestors, helped us celebrate the pioneer sesquicentennial, and got tons of free worldwide publicity for the church."

The town of Bluffdale has agreed to host an annual Days of '97 parade, and a symposium on the 1997 pioneers will be held later this year, to be followed by publication of a commemorative volume. The committee is still searching for a suitable site for a large granite-and-brass monument.

Local Man Arrested for Following Prophet
By Terrill W. Cannon

SALT LAKE CITY—A restraining order has been issued to keep local resident Doug Atwater at least 300 yards away from LDS Church president Gordon B. Hinckley at all times.

Atwater claimed he was only doing what he had learned in Primary, to which the Salt Lake district attorney replied, "Did they tell you to follow the prophet in a Lincoln Town Car with the lights off?" Atwood admitted they had not, but he added, "They never said I couldn't, either."

Neither the church nor Atwater were available for comment.

American Medical Association Protests Priesthood Blessings
By Terrill W. Cannon

BOSTON, MA—In a statement issued this week by the American Medical Association, the physician group protested the use of LDS priesthood blessings for the treatment of disease or injury.

Spokesperson Nan Doerty indicated that the lack of empirical evidence supporting the efficacy of priesthood blessings and the fact that LDS priesthood holders generally lack the proper training and licensure for the practice of medicine anywhere in North America could result in greater harm than good for patients.

When asked if LDS physicians would be cleared to use the priesthood to heal the sick, Doerty indicated that they could probably "get away with it," but they would be unable to bill insurance or Medicare for the procedure.

Church Allows Selected Masks in Meetinghouses
By Jack B. Kimball

SALT LAKE CITY—Because many Latter-day Saints are now holding Halloween celebrations inside church meetinghouses, the long-standing mask restrictions are being loosened.

"When someone puts on a mask, they lose their inhibitions and personal responsibility," said spokesman David Welch. "But a pilot program has shown that masks of worthy, inspiring people can actually raise the wearer's conscientiousness."

The following approved Halloween masks are now available through distribution outlets: President Hinckley, Steve Young, Stephen Covey, Gladys Knight, Marie Osmond, and Sheri Dew.

Church Adopts Multilevel Proselyting Approach

By Jack B. Kimball

SALT LAKE CITY—Facing declining rates of conversion in key markets, the church has launched a new program to motivate members to share the gospel with others and build "gospel downlines," according to spokesman Eric Nugent.

"We needed a new way to get people interested in sharing the gospel," said Nugent. "We realized that one of Utah's biggest industries is a type and a shadow of how the gospel should be spread in these last days. After all, the multilevel or network marketing industry is based upon eternal principles. Aren't we all part of God's downline, with commissions of glory flowing to him for all our righteous deeds? He's the great Diamond Distributor in the sky."

The way the new program works is that whenever a church member sponsors a new member into the gospel, member A will receive a ten-percent commission on all tithing paid by new member B. In turn, when member B brings in new convert C, both A and B will receive ten percent of C's tithing. This commission plan continues up to eight levels deep.

"It's time to start inviting people over for dinner under mysterious pretenses and then spring the gospel plan on them," says spokesman Nugent. "This program will help with the church's retention and reactivation efforts too, since the more tithing your downline pays, the more blessings you'll receive. Of course, you're expected to pay tithing on your commissions."

Members who sponsor 20 new converts will receive an exclusive lapel pin featuring a sparkly sunstone. Members who sponsor 15 new converts receive a moonstone lapel pin, and those who sponsor 10 new converts receive a starstone pin.

"Aren't we all part of God's downline, with commissions of glory flowing to him for all our righteous deeds?"

High-level achievers can earn even greater rewards, according to the new plan. Members who sponsor 100 new converts may take two pieces of bread and two cups of water when the sacrament tray comes around. Members who break the 500-convert threshold earn the coveted Family Home Evening Exemption Pass, which excuses them from the church's weekly in-home program. And those who crack the 1,000-convert mark receive all the tokens and signs required to gain entrance to the VIP luxury box at LaVell Edwards Stadium for every BYU Cougar home game.

In order for the new multilevel proselyting plan to function at full Zion capacity, those participating in the program must pay tithing at 25 percent, effective immediately.

Area Man Alleges General Conference Reruns

SPRINGVILLE, UT—Melvin Fingdingler of the Springville 13th Ward believes that the church has been showing old reruns of general conference during April and October for the past several years.

According to Fingdingler, the realization came when, this past April, he awoke briefly from his nap to hear the monotone words of a talk he was almost sure he had heard before.

"I thought I was dreaming until I distinctly heard the speaker say, 'I lift thee and thou lift me, and we both will rise together,'" explained Fingdingler. "That line piqued my curiosity, since I was almost positive I'd heard the same speaker say it with the same intonation years ago."

Fingdingler began rummaging through the old general conference videotapes that his wife keeps next to the Living Scripture videos under the television. Upon reviewing a conference tape from April 1997, he confirmed his theory that the church is just rerunning old general conferences.

"My first thought was, why hasn't anyone else noticed this yet?" Fingdingler remarked. "But then I began to think about it and just decided that, you know, it's all good. Read your scriptures, be good, say your prayers, et cetera. How many times can you change up those themes in an effort to make them sound interesting? Please. These men may have the priesthood, but they're not magicians."

Fingdingler called church headquarters to inquire about the reruns. He said he was given the runaround by a secretary who declined to give her name. She did, however, end the awkward phone call by explaining to Fingdingler her own opinion as to why the church began showing conference reruns.

"I think at first the church would rotate the same talk themes every few years, but then they just kind of thought, what's the point?" said the secretary. "It's kind of like the whole sealed portion of the Book of Mormon thing, you know? We'll never get the sealed portion until we're living the doctrine already revealed. I guess we still haven't incorporated that talk about member missionary work from 1998, so the church just decided to keep showing it until we do."

Snapshot

It's rare for the church to speak out on controversies. What recent issues have church spokespeople declined to comment on?

The absence of cup holders in the new Conference Center seats

The fact that you can say "brethren" but not "sistren"

Whether one-piece garments are holier than two-piece

Bunions

The sudden popularity of fish tacos

Whether or not those little plastic things on the end of shoelaces have a name

What the heck happened to make *Saturday Night Live* so sucky

Who put the ram in the ramalamadingdong

Humanitarian Efforts Lead to Fewer Saved Souls

SALT LAKE CITY—Following last week's report of sharply declining admissions to the celestial kingdom, the *Enquirer* uncovered evidence that the devil himself is influencing self-proclaimed "humanitarian" groups like the World Health Organization to promote sanitation, rehydration therapies, and vaccines in cholera-stricken third-world countries.

Millions of children, mostly under age five, die annually in impoverished parts of Africa and Asia due to infectious diarrhea, an easily treatable condition. All these little children are "alive in Christ," so they are admitted directly into the celestial kingdom. But with growing international efforts to prevent such deaths, more children are surviving, and fewer and fewer children each year are being received into God's highest glory.

"The scriptures have warned of those who extend physical aid with one hand while slashing chances for salvation with the other."

"The adversary will do anything in his power to keep each of these precious souls from receiving salvation, and many of the elect have been deceived," said BYU sociologist Howard Everson, who agrees with the *Enquirer*'s findings. "The scriptures have warned of such latter-day wolves in sheep's clothing, those who extend physical aid with one hand while slashing chances for salvation with the other."

Everson believes the LDS Church should immediately withdraw all financial support from such relief organizations, in hopes of slowing or reversing the downward trend in gross salvation numbers. He estimates that the church could increase entries into the celestial kingdom by a hundred or more souls per $1,000 of donations withheld.

"It's a win-win situation for Heavenly Father's plan," Everson said. "It means more souls saved and more money available for church-produced movies."

Church Swaps Mall for Pacific Island
By Milton P. Romney

SALT LAKE CITY—The LDS Church announced that it has swapped Crossroads Mall in downtown Salt Lake City for the island of Tonga.

During a public meeting held in Tonga, church officials assured non-Mormon islanders that little would change, except for the "deplorable" dress standards.

"We can move the entire royal family, plus our cows, to the mall in a little less than six months," said Tongan prince Fu'uatama. "Most of our people are pretty excited about the food court."

Though it's not clear what the church has in mind for the island, all the General Authorities will travel to Tonga next month to "determine its purpose in the kingdom."

Stake Starts Using Sacrament Meeting Safety Script

By Teancum Zenos Smoot IV

CEDAR CITY, UT—According to stake president James Davila, all units throughout the Cedar Breaks Stake are now required to read the following safety script aloud at the beginning of each sacrament meeting:

Welcome to sacrament service. We hope your experience will be an enjoyable one. In order to make your meeting as comfortable as possible, we want to acquaint you with the safety features of this building.

Four clearly marked exits have been provided for your convenience. Please take a moment to find the one nearest to you. Remember that it may be behind you. Please walk, do not run, to the exit if there are more than three youth speakers on the program.

> **"Your seat bottom can be used as a floatation device should Sister Burkenheim bear her testimony."**

In the unlikely event of a high council speaker, air masks will drop from the ceiling. Place the mouthpiece over your mouth, and extend the strap over your head. Although the bag may not appear to inflate, the stimulant will be flowing. Help your children with their masks before securing your own. You may remove the masks when the speaker is finished or the meeting is over, which ever comes later.

Your seat bottom can be used as a floatation device should Sister Burkenheim bear her testimony. Simply remove the cushion, sweep away the Cheerios, and put your arms through the straps on the back.

Remember, Coke consumption is prohibited for the duration of the meeting. Federal law prohibits disabling or destroying the lavatory Coke detectors.

As the meeting progresses, our deacons will be coming through with snack and beverage service. Please keep the aisle clear for them. At the end of the meeting, we ask that you put your teenagers back into their upright, locked position and stow all belongings in your church bags.

Have a great meeting, and thanks for picking the LDS Church for all your spiritual needs.

Fasting Requirements Loosened

By Jack B. Kimball

SALT LAKE CITY—To relieve the burden of going without food and water for 24 consecutive hours, members are now allowed to split up their fasting into smaller periods of time. Some members are calling the new approach "fast fasting."

"As long as the total fasting comes out to 24 hours per month, the blessings are the same," said Elder Jeff W. Richards. "A member could open his fast with prayer, go without food and water for an hour or two, and then close with prayer. In fact, a fasting period could last as little as just a few seconds, as long as it opens and closes with prayer."

Susan Pugmire, a member in Sandy, Utah, applauds the change. "Now we won't have to deal with headaches and bad breath," she says. "I like this new kinder, gentler direction. Life is already hard enough without excessively long fasts."

To help members track their fasting throughout the month, fasting time cards are now available at distribution centers.

Predictions for the Future

Scrapbooking will pass agriculture and tourism to become the second-largest industry in Utah.

Ward Clamps Down on Testimony Requirements

By Kylee-Ashlee Cannon Christiansen

ALPINE, UT—In an attempt to make sure the bearing of testimonies is "as uplifting and enlightening as possible," Bishop Gerrald R. Schwartz of the Alpine 34th Ward has created "a few helpful guidelines" for people to use when they want to bear their testimonies.

After the church gave guidelines about what topics should be discussed when bearing testimonies, such as the truth of the church and the role of Joseph Smith, Bishop Schwartz says, "I began to see how sacred testimony-bearing time really is. I started to realize that I had a crucial duty to make sure that time was used correctly."

After church officials explained that children should not be encouraged to bear their testimonies in sacrament meeting, Bishop Schwartz began to fast and pray about the topic. "When the Brethren began to emphasize that testimonies are not travelogues and that people shouldn't use that time to tell long personal stories, I began to see that the members in my ward needed some help," he explained.

Consequently, he created the following testimony waiver, which members must sign each fast and testimony day if they want to bear their testimonies:

Your Name:
Your Bishop's Name:
Your Baptism Number:

In order to bear your testimony today, you must conform to the following guidelines:

1. *You must be between the ages of 18 and 45. This is because the Brethren have asked that no children bear their testimonies in sacrament meeting and, frankly, old people tend to ramble.*

2. *You must be male. Women cry too much.*

3. *If you are over 25, you must be married. Otherwise, you are a menace to others' testimonies.*

4. *You must be appropriately attired in a suit, white shirt, and conservative tie, and you should be wearing your "I Passed the Tie Check!" sticker. These stickers are awarded in the foyer ten minutes before sacrament meeting starts.*

5. *You must be a native English speaker. Accents detract from the Spirit.*

6. *You must agree to read the following script when bearing your testimony. Items 6a and 6c are mandatory; item 6b is optional. You must choose only two sentences from 6b, but you may decide in which order to say them.*

a. *MANDATORY: My dear brothers and sisters, I am glad to stand before you on this [warm, sunny, stormy, windy] day and bear my heartfelt testimony. I know this church is true. [You may also say: I know the LDS Church is true]. I know Joseph Smith is a prophet. I know the Book of Mormon is true. And I know Gordon B. Hinckley is a prophet. [You may also say: I know President Hinckley is a prophet.]*

b. *OPTIONAL (choose two): I have a testimony of prayer. I have a testimony of fasting. I have a testimony of church attendance. I have a testimony of temple attendance. I have a testimony that families are forever. I have a testimony of tithing. I have a testimony of the Word of Wisdom. I have a testimony of the Law of Chastity. I have a testimony that all R-rated movies are bad. I have a testimony that our church leaders are called of God and everything they do is righteous. I have a testimony of obedience.*

c. MANDATORY:
In the name of Jesus Christ, amen.

I have read and understood the terms as described above. I realize that if I misrepresent myself or vary from the above script, such actions will have severe repercussions on my standing in the church.

Applicant's Signature:

WOWPD Blotter

3:04 p.m.
Routine screening of state liquor store customers.
Three temple recommends: **CONFISCATED**

4:19 p.m.
Cornered known repeat offender in Target parking lot. Beer most likely hidden beneath vegetables in his grocery bag. However, while giving chase, officer got weary and fainted. Suspect escaped.

5:13 p.m.
Hot day. Gave speech at annual 145th Ward barbecue on evils of breaking WoW. Enjoyed five burgers, potato chips, root beer, company of the righteous. Went to check out nearby picnic involving a bottle of wine. One temple recommend: **CONFISCATED**

Know Your Mormon Terms

Teen Commandments: What the church dictates to youth regarding what they can wear, when they can date, what they can watch at the movies, where they can touch each other, etc.

Views from the Street

What are your favorite general conference traditions?

"My boyfriend and I like to go to Temple Square to feel the Spirit and make out on the lawn."

"I make bets with my roommates on whether one woman will speak or two."

Corrections

We regret to inform readers that our "exclusive" interview with President Hinckley in the August 16th issue wasn't exclusive—in fact, it wasn't even real. An *Enquirer* reporter admitted she made the entire thing up. "Except for the part where President Hinckley said my calling and election have been made sure—he definitely said that," the reporter claimed. Appropriate disciplinary action has been taken.

Members are advised to stop sending empty pizza boxes to the Humanitarian Sort Center, as previously instructed by the *Enquirer*. The church is no longer using pizza boxes to build temporary shelters in underprivileged and disaster areas. Volunteers have discovered that victims don't appreciate being constantly exposed to the lingering odors of cheese, pepperoni, and tomato sauce.

Ward Shares Stories of Inspiring Pioneer Ancestors

By Teancum Zenos Smoot IV

HEBER CITY, UT—Fast and testimony meeting in the Heber Heights Fourth Ward was especially inspiring this past month, according to many who attended.

"The theme seemed to be our pioneer ancestors," said Sally Luhan. "Sister Yount started it all when she told a story about her great-great-great-aunt who crossed the plains with her family. Her ancestor had even heard Joseph Smith preach. I could tell she was very proud of the faith and dedication of her forebears."

After Sister Yount, others also praised their pioneer ancestors. "My great-great-great-grandfather single-handedly pulled a handcart from Iowa City to Salt Lake City," said Brother Harold Jones, tears welling in his eyes.

Sister Felicia Smart told of her great-great-great-grandmother, who had a baby at Nauvoo just as the Saints were driven out. She gave birth to another in Winter Quarters and another on the way to Salt Lake City, where she had another baby just before she and her husband were called to settle Panguitch, Utah, where she bore triplets.

Continuing in the spirit of the meeting, Brother Thornton Ratt recounted the trials of his great-great-great-great-grandfather. "After miraculously surviving a suicide mission to protect the prophet Joseph Smith, Grandpa Ratt, laid low with botulism, loaded his wife and seven children onto a handcart, all of them paralyzed from polio, and pulled them toward Zion. On the way a wheel broke, so he pushed the cart the rest of the way on one wheel." Brother Ratt could no longer contain his sobs when he described how his noble ancestor lived the rest of his life without hands or toenails as a result of these trials.

The spirit of the meeting continued to climb when Sister Maxine Smiley related a story about her great-great-great-cousin six times removed who was blind but nevertheless learned to play "Come, Come Ye Saints" on the mouth harp.

> **One sister's pioneer ancestor drew up the architectural plans for the Church Office Building using the original Urim and Thummim.**

"Though she was blind, my great ancestor did many noble things," Smiley said. "She was the fourteenth wife of Joseph Smith and single-handedly painted the intricate mural on the ceiling of the Nauvoo temple." Smiley's ancestor went on to foil a plot by the CIA to assassinate Brigham Young and deport all Mormons to El Salvador, predict the assassination of John F. Kennedy, carry an ailing ox for a destitute Danish family from Winter Quarters to Salt Lake City, and draw up the architectural plans for the Church Office Building using the original Urim and Thummim employed by King Mosiah to translate the Jaredite records.

Then, at age 75, Sister Smiley's blind forebear, with the aid of only a single-shot rifle and a hatchet, stopped a band of 70 murderous Mexican banditos from destroying the Mormon colonies. As the battle ended, she was seen walking toward a pillar of light with three men "dressed after the manner of the Nephites."

"It was quite a testimony meeting," said Bishop Vanguard. "Some of the stories reminded me of one of my own pioneer ancestors. He was the first to bring Mormonism to the headhunters of the Congo. Of course, that was after he masterminded Joseph Smith's presidential campaign and the formation of the secret council of One Hundred and Forty-Four, which has since infiltrated international politics and was responsible for bringing Saddam Hussein to justice."

Girls No Longer Allowed to Sing Missionary Song
By Jack B. Kimball

BOUNTIFUL, UT—Four adjacent stakes in this heavily Mormon suburb have joined together to prohibit young females from singing the popular Primary song "I Hope They Call Me on a Mission."

"Too many of our young women are still behaving as if the Lord expects them to serve missions," said Bountiful East Bench stake president Curt Patterson. "The prophet has made it clear that girls don't need to serve missions and shouldn't feel any obligation. This song is indoctrinating our young ladies otherwise."

The song is still being sung in Primaries throughout the stakes, but only by the boys. "For now, we're asking the girls to reverently bow their heads during this song and keep their mouths shut," says stake Primary music director Linda Willis. "We're thinking about writing alternative lyrics for them to sing. We've already got a first line: 'I hope he asks me to get married, when I have grown a cup size or two.'"

Snapshot

Things That Seem Like They Would Be Funny, But Are Not

- Using grilled cheese sandwiches for the sacrament

- Slipping into Relief Society and loudly telling any random old lady that you found her diaphragm

- Solemnly appointing high priests to be captains of fifty for the march to Jackson County

- Sending a letter to all the Laurels saying they can wear whatever they want to girls' camp

- Telling the priests they can serve as priesthood chaperones at girls' camp

- Standing to bear your testimony, then falling to the ground screaming and wrestling with an unseen demon

- Telling the nursery leader that, like an apostle, her calling is for life

- Tie-dyeing your garments

- Telling the choir director to include a drum solo in the next Easter program

- Whispering to that pimply-faced deacon that you know the real reason he had to get glasses

- Dumping your fiancée because she's not physically fit enough to make the walk to Missouri

Chapter 7:
Jots & Tittles of Scripture

D id you know Mormon scripture tote bags have ancient origins? That the popular *Work and the Glory* historical fiction series is being republished in a special scripture-quality edition? That the sealed portion of the golden plates has been found aboard the Titanic wreck?

If you didn't know about these important developments in the field of Mormon scriptures, the *Enquirer* comes to your rescue. The Book of Mormon may be the most correct book on earth, but the *Enquirer* reports the most correct news. In fact, there's even a scripture about us: "Those men that did bring up the evil report upon the land, died by the plague before the Lord" (*Num. 14: 37*). Wait a minute—wrong scripture. Here's the right one: "A good report maketh the bones fat" (*Prov. 15: 30*).

New Foundation Seeks Origins of Scripture Tote Bags

SALT LAKE CITY—Clark Herzmann, president of Scripture Luggage, Inc., the premier manufacturer of Mormon scripture tote bags, announced today the formation of a new Mormon research organization, the Foundation for Ancient Research on Toting Scriptures.

"Now, more than ever, the use of scripture tote bags is under subtle and insidious attack by so-called intellectual and liberal Mormons," said Herzmann at a press conference. "They prefer to simply carry their scriptures rather than use the more traditional scripture tote, and they frequently deride those who prefer leatherette, handled bags. The purpose of the foundation is to, first, demonstrate the antiquity of scripture tote bags with rigorous historical research, and second, fully restore the former dignity of the venerable usage of tote bags for transporting divine writ."

"The use of scripture tote bags is under subtle and insidious attack by so-called intellectual and liberal Mormons."

According to Martin Schlaggle, the newly hired research director at the Foundation for Ancient Research on Toting Scriptures, tote bags were used by ancient Hebrews and Christians. "Yes, the form of the tote might have changed from dispensation to dispensation, but its function was never altered," he said. Schlaggle is a professor of Middle Eastern studies at the University of Utah.

"Look at the big jars the Dead Sea Scrolls were buried in," continued Schlaggle. "We have significant archeological evidence that these jars were actually used for carrying and storing scrolls. And, don't forget the ancient

Israelite practice of wearing phylacteries on the forehead. No one disputes that those headbands had a little pouch in the front specifically designed to carry scriptures."

To promote the Foundation for Ancient Research on Toting Scriptures, Scripture Luggage has announced a new line of scripture totes that Herzman hopes will soon become collector items. Herzman describes the new product as a "kind of modern version of the Jewish phylactery that we call the Mormon Prophylactery. It's a stylish headband with a pocket in the front large enough to carry a small-print scripture quad, along with small loops on the sides to carry markers. It's made of genuine leather and will protect not only the scriptures but also the forehead."

Herzman ended the press conference by saying, "We take this opportunity to request that when members of the press refer to the Foundation for Ancient Research on Toting Scriptures, they use the full name of our organization for the initial reference. If an abbreviated reference is necessary thereafter, our foundation should be simply referred to as the foundation. Unlike other Mormon research foundations such as FARMS and FAIR, we request that members of the press not use any acronyms in referring to the foundation."

Predictions for the Future

A general authority will refer to Harry Potter in general conference, thus making him part of Mormon scripture.

Scripture-Quality Edition of *Work and the Glory* to Be Released

By M. Spencer Pratt

SALT LAKE CITY—Deseret Book announced that the wildly popular *Work and the Glory* series will be released in a scripture-quality edition. The volumes will feature black or brown leather covers, gilt edges, extensive cross-referencing with the standard works, ribbon bookmarks, chapter index tabs, and a two-column chapter-verse format. Also planned is a line of carrying cases designed to be worn as backpacks that will hold all ten volumes and still leave enough room for a quadruple combination. Deseret Book officials declined to comment on rumored plans for a tetradecauple combination.

"We are merely attempting to make this landmark series more accessible to the LDS public by putting it into a format they are already used to reading," said Deseret Book spokesman Mark White. "We are in no way attempting to campaign for the series to be declared part of the standard works to boost sales. Really ... we promise."

"Those books are like so totally spiritual!"

Despite this assurance, however, rumors of the series' imminent canonization have already begun to spread.

"Omigosh!" said local Beehive Mandi Meecham. "When I heard the news, I was like so excited I couldn't even believe it! I've heard those books are like so totally spiritual! I mean, I couldn't get all the way through the first book because it was so long, but I know my friend Britni's mother read them, and they like totally helped her testimony, you know? It's so cool they're finally going to be scriptures now!"

Snapshot

What will we ask when we reach the spirit world?

What's the grossest thing I ever ate without knowing it?

Who decided organ music was more reverent than bongos?

What's the deal with women?

Who's the most famous dead person whose bodily molecule became part of my own body?

Who's the most attractive person who secretly liked me?

How many pedophiles did I shake hands with?

Did I ever use a product made from recycled materials that contained matter from a product I'd previously used?

How come dogs include tiny, yappy animals and also huge, scary ones, while all pet cats are the same size?

If all my fingernail and toenail clippings were gathered in one pile, how big would it be?

Whoa! Did anyone get the license plate of that truck? And, hey, what's with all the clouds?

Franklin Covey Materials Found in Al-Qaeda Training Camps
By Terrill W. Cannon

KANDAHAR, AFGHANISTAN—In a press briefing today, Secretary of Defense Donald Rumsfeld detailed the discovery in Al-Qaeda facilities of LDS organizational guru Stephen Covey's book *The Seven Habits of Highly Effective People* and other items, including a number of Franklin Planners and Palm organizers.

Special Forces units working to secure various Taliban and Al-Qaeda strongholds discovered the Covey materials packed in watertight ammunition boxes along with other papers, a copy of the Koran, and a half-dozen mercury switches.

"Clearly this information was of great importance to the terrorists," Rumsfeld reported. Walls of the cave were covered in Arabic slogans that read: "Seek first to understand ... then to be understood," "Synergize," and "Begin with the end in mind."

"Their 'Production of Desired Results' is completely misaligned with their 'Production Capability.'"

Lyell Johnson, a spokesperson for Franklin Covey, said that the terrorists seem to be suffering from a P/PC problem. "Their 'Production of Desired Results' is completely misaligned with their 'Production Capability.' And that's a pretty serious threat to their access to any kind of public success."

Military language experts indicate that the papers found in the stronghold seem to be an attempt to translate *Seven Habits* into Arabic for distribution to any number of terrorist cells. Further work will be necessary before the translations can be confirmed, though sources at the Pentagon indicate that the translators seemed to be struggling to dissociate the principles from the Western/corporate paradigm of the infidels.

Hofmann Forgeries Now More Valuable Than Originals
By Teancum Zenos Smoot IV

SALT LAKE CITY—A rough draft for one of the notorious Salamander Letters, forgeries of letters supposedly from the LDS prophet Joseph Smith but in reality created by Mark Hofmann, recently sold at public auction for more than an original letter written by Joseph Smith himself.

Howard Mumford, the winner of the forgery, is proud of his purchase. "Which would you prefer, I ask you?" he said. "A laundry list from the prophet, or a forged letter that led to bombings, death, destruction, and apostasy?"

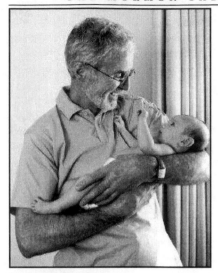

Names May Be Linguistic Clue to Adamic Language
By David Patton Benson

PROVO, UT—Scholars in BYU's Adamic Linguistics Department have confirmed that they are investigating the "inspired" first names given by Ephraim M. Featherstone to his children. The scholars believe these names may offer possible clues to the vocabulary and grammar of the original, pure language spoken by Adam in the Garden of Eden, as well as in heaven.

In a press conference, Professor LaVerdon P. Dibble said, "We're convinced that the names given by Brother Featherstone to his fourteen children may well have roots in the Adamic tongue. They're certainly not like anything found on our planet in its current, telestial state."

For over thirty years, Featherstone, a claims adjuster and high priest residing in the Magna Utah Eighteenth Ward, has relied on inspiration to name his children. "It's the most amazing thing," said Featherstone's bishop, Merwin C. Breinholt. "Ephraim just stands there, bouncing the baby up and down like all of us do. Only when he does it, you can just feel inspiration coming over him. And then, he not only gives the child the name but explains what it means." He added, "Our ward has been richly blessed."

Featherstone's wife, WaLonna, says that her husband's unusual gift first manifested itself during the naming of the couple's first child. "We had pretty much decided to name him Michael, after my father," she said. "But then, as Ephraim started giving the blessing, he got this inspiration, and next thing you know the baby's named Gleed. I was a little miffed at first, but then Ephraim said the name means 'faithful and holy' in Adamic."

Although a number of ward members commented on the inspirational character of Featherstone's blessings, attempts to interview Featherstone's children regarding their unusual names were less successful. Neither Gleed nor Thone ("prayerful") Featherstone, the couple's two oldest children, would return phone calls. Fwalti ("expert canner") Featherstone responded with a brusque "no comment" to a request for an interview. And a child playing in the Featherstone front yard, believed to be Naxaltiles ("valiant until the end of time") Featherstone, insisted that his first name was actually Brad.

> **"As Ephraim started giving the blessing, he got this inspiration, and next thing you know the baby's named Gleed."**

Featherstone downplays the significance of his children's names. "I don't consider my spiritual gifts beyond what any mortal could attain to," he said. "I'm just a humble conduit."

New PDA Plug-In Broadcasts Scripture-Study Habits

SALT LAKE CITY—This week, Franklin-Covey released a software plug-in that works with LDS scripture applications on electronic handheld devices such as the Palm Pilot. Called Rameumptom 2.1, the program features a voice message that announces, "You've just opened your scriptures" whenever a user accesses the standard works on his or her PDA.

The new program is being met with rave reviews. "Rameumptom is absolutely a heaven-sent gift," attested Bishop William McCann. "Because some people use their Palms to play games during church, we righteous folk need a way to let everyone know we're actually reading the scriptures on ours."

"It helps everyone know I'm not playing Tetris."

Local elders quorum president Brandon Mills echoed Bishop McCann's sentiments. "People need to trust me and my inherent goodness, especially as I'm in a position of leadership," he said. "The Rameumptom 2.1 helps me project the right image when I turn on my Palm Pilot in Sunday school. And it helps everyone know I'm not playing Tetris, like my wife does. She's always trying to break her high score when she thinks I'm not looking."

Franklin-Covey's Rameumptom 2.1 features several customization options. When Burt Landgren, an area stake president, opens the Book of Mormon on his PDA, he hears President Hinckley's voice say, "Brother Landgren, you have opened your e-scriptures 1,257 times." Landgren likes to set the voice on maximum volume.

Although the program received high marks from men, women seem to like it too. "I don't own a Palm Pilot because I'm too stupid for technology," laughed area Relief Society president Joan Burke. "But I'm so humbly grateful for the Rameumptom. My husband's PDA is a real temptation for him because he likes to pretend he's looking up a scripture when he's really just playing Space Invaders. But this program keeps him honest. Maybe now he'll finally get to be a bishop."

Rumors that techno-savvy consumers have found ways to hack the Rameumptom application and make it work when a game or other non-scriptural program is opened are as yet unverified.

Petitioners Want Old Testament Removed from Standard Works

MESA, AZ—Citing the Old Testament's excessive violence, sexual situations, and foul language, members of the Mesa Twenty-Third Ward have been circulating a petition to eliminate the Old Testament from the standard works. The move was precipitated by Sister Hannah Swenson, who became aware of the "R-rated material" in the Old Testament while reading 1 Kings to her children.

She was shocked to discover the word *pisseth* repeated numerous times throughout the book. "There is rape and murder and incest in those stories, but the toilet talk was the straw that broke the camel's back," Swenson said. "Until I can get Salt Lake to listen, it's going to be those *Davey and Goliath* cartoons for my kids. We'll just leave that Old Testament on the shelf until after the kids are married."

Views from the Street

What do you think the celestial kingdom will be like?

"I just want to know if our spirit children will require diaper changes and 3 a.m. feedings."

"I plan on continuing to grow and progress until not even my mother-in-law can find fault with me."

"I hope we still have to pee, because I think it feels real nice to pee."

"I can think of several single women who I hope get assigned to me as plural wives."

"I'm assuming that my reward for a lifetime of self-denial and control will be an eternal orgy of self-indulgence and pleasure."

"I hope I gain a cup size or two in the resurrection."

Book of Mormon Blesses Area Man's Life

By Jack B. Kimball

LINCOLN, NE—Amos Tanner always knew the Book of Mormon would bring him blessings. "This book is like a treasure that was buried just for me, and I only needed to exercise the faith to dig it up," says the fifth-generation Latter-day Saint.

After Tanner's father died recently, he and his two surviving siblings cleaned out the house. To everyone's surprise, Amos discovered a first-edition copy of the Book of Mormon in the attic. Appraisers found that the book was in better condition than any previously known copy.

"When we sold it for $90,000 and I received my one-third share, my heart just burst with faith and gratitude," Tanner said. "Surely this scripture was laid up in store for our time. Now I can finally buy that motor home."

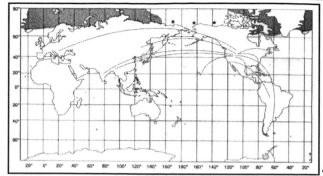

New Microchip Tracks Seventies' Migration Patterns

By Teancum Zenos Smoot IV

SALT LAKE CITY—Tracing their origins to the New Testament, Seventies are charged with spreading the gospel throughout the world. As the first year of a new Seventies tracking program winds up, scientists are trying to interpret the information they've received from tiny microchips planted in the earlobes of newly called members of all Quorums of the Seventy.

The study, performed by sociologists and wildlife biologists at the University of Illinois Urbana and funded by the U.S. Department of Wildlife, has successfully gathered transmissions from the microchips about the whereabouts of the Seventies.

"It was a question that frankly had the whole nation puzzled," said Dr. Tim Miner, head of the project. "A slew of new Seventies would be introduced at general conference, and then we'd never hear from them again until about five years later, when they'd show up to be released."

The burning question, Miner stated, was, "Where on earth do these brethren disappear to?"

To answer that question, scientists applied a local anesthetic and inserted a microchip into the earlobe of each Seventy as he left the Conference Center after general conference.

During the next year, the scientists used sophisticated instruments to track the position of each Seventy all over the globe.

"It was a time-consuming task," admitted Dean Heaton, head of the surveillance team. "Those guys are all over the place. And sometimes the microchips would malfunction and we'd have to track the guy down. But wouldn't you know it, in most cases not even their wives knew where they were."

"In all my years of studying migration patterns, I have never seen a species so given to world travel."

When worse came to worst, the tracking team had to chase down an errant Seventy in a helicopter and shoot him with tranquilizer darts in order to insert a new microchip. "Sometimes we'd catch one in the middle of a sermon and have to down him in front of all those people," said Heaton. "He'd get kinda groggy and incoherent, but no one really seemed to notice."

Miner says the data they've gathered so far is yet to be interpreted. "All I can say is that, in all my years of studying the migration pattern of humpback whales and ribboned seals, I have never seen a species so given to world travel," he said. "Our initial findings show intense activity in Jackson County, Missouri; Jerusalem; and Cancun, Mexico. We have theories about the goings on in the first two places, but we're baffled by Cancun. Is there a temple there or something?"

Dinosaur National Monument Secedes from Utah

By Milton P. Romney

VERNAL, UT—The roughly fifty square miles of Dinosaur National Monument, situated for years on the border of eastern Utah, seceded from the state last week and joined neighboring Colorado.

Citing irreconcilable differences with the Mormons of Utah, the paleontologists and staff of Dinosaur National Monument express relief to finally be accepted by people whose ideology includes the recognition that creatures lived and died on the earth prior to the Garden of Eden six thousand years ago.

Vernal stake president Levon Patterson, said, "Good. Colorado can have 'em. Never have I seen people so deceived by the adversary as the employees of the so-called Dinosaur National Monument."

Typo Exacerbates Anti-Church Sentiment

BUSHLAND, TX—A weekly bible quotation on the outdoor message board of the First Baptist Church of Bushland reads, "You can't love God and Mormon."

According to First Baptist's pastor, Tom Davenport, the sign was supposed to read, "You can't love God and Mammon," but evidently the deacon in charge had some trouble reading Pastor Davenport's instructions.

The deacon, who asked to remain anonymous, denies the charge of illiteracy, saying, "That's the message the Lord wanted on our church, and I'll fight any man in the county to keep it there."

Predictions for the Future

The Temple Department will suddenly remember that Pres. Hinckley announced a temple for Wyoming five years ago.

Disney will open a Book of Mormon theme ride based on the Jaredite barges.

Three Nephite Identities Revealed

By David Patton Benson

PROVO, UT—The current earthly identities of three apostles mentioned in the Book of Mormon, commonly known as the Three Nephites, will soon be revealed, the *Enquirer* has learned. After three decades of research, a team of theomusicologists discovered that the legendary Nephites are in fact the seminal musical group the Bee Gees. After protracted negotiations, the Nephite musicians have decided to go public.

"We finally decided it was time to reveal ourselves," Maurice Gibb told the *Enquirer*. "We knew there was a chance people would find out anyway, when the *Saturday Night Fever* soundtrack went double platinum a while back. Personally, I'm glad to put aside the hoax about my death and the name Maurice altogether. I'm really Mathonihah, brother of Mathoni. Barry's Mathoni, by the way."

"I'm a little surprised that no one picked up on it earlier," Kumenonhi (a.k.a. Robin Gibb) told our reporter. "We put enough clues in our songs. I mean, that repeated chorus where we just kept saying 'Staying alive, staying alive?' What did you think we were talking about? 'Tragedy' is obviously about the fall of the Nephite civilization. And 'How Deep Is Your Love'? Did no one get that we were talking about the atonement?"

Apparently, the lyrics were only part of the puzzle that researchers Steve Rucker and Alan Kendall put together. "What really cinched it for us was our audio-graphic work," said Rucker. "Most human voices are incapable of reaching more than 8,000 cycles per second, or hertz. But the Bee Gees' voices top out at over 15,000 ▶

Your compensation for failure in the home: Mozac™

115

hertz. Only terrestrial beings are capable of making such sounds."

"Our song 'Tragedy' is obviously about the fall of the Nephite civilization. Did no one get that?"

Rucker and Kendall say that the real mystery is why, after two thousand years, the Three Nephites would choose to publicly reveal themselves now. But Mathonihah says it's really no mystery. "We just got tired, that's all. Helping stranded motorists, rescuing lost children—it wears you down after awhile. The life of a pop star had some real appeal. Artists want their work to last, and we really can go on forever."

Mormon Community Awards

Most efficient, timely food storage rotation: Kelly Jones, Anaheim, CA

Shortest testimony that still managed to include every single cliché: Kristen Griffiths, Medford, MA

Lifetime award for the most consecutive Republican votes: LaVell Hickens, age 96, Nephi, UT

Snapshot

What attention grabbers are we using to begin our talks and lessons?

"I'd like to perform my dance interpretation of the Willey and Martin Handcart Companies."

"As Nostradamus once said . . ."

"To dramatize how important the Word of Wisdom is, I'm going to light up one of these old stogies."

"I'd like to begin by reading a passage from a book of scripture I wrote myself."

"As I sat on the toilet last night, my thoughts turned to the purging process of repentance."

"I'd like to sing you my testimony of food storage."

"Since I don't have a testimony, I'll take this opportunity to share some grievances I have with the church."

Sealed Portion of Golden Plates Recovered from Titanic Wreck

By Jack B. Kimball

REYKJAVIK, ICELAND—The operators of an Icelandic research ship have recovered the sealed portion of the golden plates from the wreck of the Titanic and returned it to the church, in exchange for funds to offset costs.

"I was the one who recognized the find," said Icelandic crewman and church member Hálfdan Helgason, through an interpreter. "The plates were hidden in what was originally a crate of silk textiles. The three-ring metal binder contained no loose plates, only a stack of plates sealed with a band. Unlike most of the artifacts we've recovered, the plates didn't show any signs of corrosion or age."

Although no single source was able to offer a complete explanation for why the plates were aboard the doomed ship, the Enquirer has pieced together the story.

After Joseph Smith translated the unbound portion of the plates, the angel Moroni reclaimed only the loose plates and left the sealed portion in the church's possession, although the church always claimed that all the plates had been repossessed. During the early 1850s, a group of disgruntled former Mormons in Salt Lake City learned that the church was still harboring the sealed portion. After several attempts by this group to infiltrate church headquarters, authorities decided to secretly send the plates to England with Parley P. Pratt for safekeeping and possible preliminary translation work. Eventually the plates were buried on undisclosed church property in Liverpool. In the early 1900s, church authorities decided it was time to recall them.

However, the person selected to escort the plates back to Salt Lake City made the ill-fated choice to sail aboard the Titanic. "I thoroughly believe the plates were meant to lie hidden for a longer time, so the Titanic sank," said a high-ranking official who voluntarily contacted the Enquirer but refused to identify himself. "It wasn't time for church headquarters to regain the plates, so the iceberg came. It's too bad the brother didn't choose an obscure cargo ship, without so many passengers."

Decades later, the discovery of the Titanic wreck resulted from inspiration, according to the source. "The time has finally arrived for the church to have the plates again," he said. "Translation has only just begun, but I can tell you beyond a shadow of a doubt that the plates do not contain instructions pertaining to the reinstitution of earthly polygamy, as some rumors say. However, cola drinkers, R-rated movie watchers, and home teaching slackers better start doing some soul-searching."

The Enquirer has learned that the Ensign magazine has been instructed to reserve ten pages per issue starting next January for "ongoing excerpts from a large, important historical document that all members must begin studying."

Other sources report that descendents of the Titanic's principal architects have seized upon this news as proof that the ship was truly indestructible, save only for acts of God.

Corrections

After several readers decoded a hidden message in a recent article exploring the LDS scriptural perspective on the ethics of houseplant care, the *Enquirer* took appropriate action against the responsible freelance reporter. To our dismay, the hidden message said: "The Jehovah's Witnesses kick the Mormons' butt." In the future, the editors will take extra caution not to allow operatives from other religions to use the *Enquirer* for their nefarious purposes.

Our article about the Utah-based Arctic Circle hamburger chain issuing a call for used plastic sacrament cups so the company could recycle them as fry-sauce containers was misreported. Under threat of legal action, the *Enquirer* pleads with overzealous readers to stop sending the little cups to Arctic Circle's corporate headquarters, even if the cups have been carefully washed and neatly stacked.

Chapter 8:
Beyond Donny & Marie

I t's well known among Mormons that Lionel Richie, Alice Cooper, Steve Martin, and several other celebrities are secretly members of the church. Oh, they may have denied it to the media, but we all know the truth.

However, did you know that Elvis Presley has accepted his posthumous baptism and that Keith Richards has rejected his? That Mormonism is poised to become Hollywood's next trendy religion, potentially to eclipse Kabbalah and perhaps even Scientology? That LDS members are now being urged to store a year's supply of entertainment along with food, clothing, and fuel?

If you've never heard these vital reports from the world of entertainment, don't despair. You can still catch up by reading the *Enquirer*'s cream-of-the-crop entertainment reportage. If there's one thing we've learned, it's that sometimes it's better to be *of* the world but not *in* it.

Gladys Knight to Release "Midnight Train to Kolob"

By Terrill W. Cannon

LAS VEGAS, NV—LDS rhythm and blues sensation Gladys Knight has returned to the recording studio to revamp her 1973 Grammy Award-winning song "Midnight Train to Georgia," this time with a Mormon spin.

"We all have a responsibility, and since I've been so wonderfully blessed, I really want to share and to make life at least a little better," Knight said. "So every chance I get to share the gospel or uplift people, I will take full advantage of that opportunity, and so I offer up my most famous song to the blessed work."

In the original version, Knight sings about a lover, but in the updated version the lyrics point to something "a little more substantial."

This world proved too much for the man
So he's leavin' the life he's come to know
He said he's goin' back to find what's left of
his world
The world he left behind not so long ago

He's leavin' on that midnight train to Kolob
Said he's goin' back to find the holier place
and time
I'll be with him on that midnight train to
Kolob
I'd rather live in his world than live without
him in mine

Knight says she hopes "Midnight Train to Kolob" might speak to her brothers and sisters in the gospel who think Kenny Rogers is funky as well as "those who know he ain't."

Elvis Presley Accepts Posthumous Baptism

By Jack B. Kimball

SPIRIT WORLD—On the twenty-fifth anniversary of his mortal death, legendary singer Elvis Presley finally accepted one of the numerous proxy baptisms performed for him in Mormon temples. In a spirit world press conference, Presley specified that he is accepting the ordinance performed by Carl Riggs in the Las Vegas Nevada Temple on August 16, 1984, the seventh anniversary of Presley's death.

"I chose Carl's baptism because he looks like me and he's won several impersonation contests," the King said in a prepared statement provided by the *Enquirer's* exclusive spirit world source. "Since Carl died in 1992, I've become friends with him and he's taught me more about the gospel. Thank you, Carl. Thank you very much."

During Presley's mortal life, the Osmond family planted the seed for his conversion by presenting him with a copy of the Book of Mormon. He reportedly read and annotated the book, making notes such as, "Must discuss with Lisa Marie."

However, Presley resisted Mormonism for the remainder of his mortal life and for many years afterward. "I thought it lacked soul," he admitted during his press conference. "The music especially was pretty unexciting. When the pills and fried peanut-butter sandwiches didn't work fast enough, I used the Mormon Tabernacle Choir to put myself to sleep."

What finally converted Presley to Mormonism was a séance-like communication he had with still-mortal black Mormon musicians Gladys Knight and Thurl Bailey. "They helped me understand that heaven knows how unappealing Mormonism's mortal music is," Presley said. "They helped me see that maybe I could be a force for good from this side of the veil."

The *Enquirer's* spirit world source said that Presley's conversion is expected to energize missionary work in the spirit world, where rates of posthumous-baptism acceptance have lagged recently at 2.3 percent.

SNAPSHOT

What Mormon-oriented reality shows are we not watching?

Choose the Mr. Right

Who Wants to Listen Reverently to a 50-Minute Lesson on Tithing?

Survivor: In the Salt Lake Temple Tunnels

American Graven Image

Fear Factor: Testimony Meeting

Joe Temple Recommend

Who Wants to Marry a Returned Missionary?

Survivor: Boy Scout Camp

LDS Filmmaker Blankets Hollywood with Pass-Along Cards
By Jack B. Kimball

HOLLYWOOD, CA — Director, screenwriter, and playwright Neil LaBute, the BYU graduate who is widely regarded as one of America's darkest, edgiest storytellers, has started showing a softer, more religious side. Throughout the L.A. film industry and the New York drama scene, LaBute is becoming known as the man who never misses an opportunity to hand out the church's pass-along cards, which contain advertisements for the church's website, a free copy of the Book of Mormon, and other proselytizing offers.

"I have to admit, I've purposely infiltrated Hollywood with an ulterior motive," LaBute told the *Enquirer*. "When I dropped the *In the Company of Men* bombshell on Sundance a few years back, I knew it would instantly buy me all kinds of credibility. I've followed that up with more dark, troubling material like *Bash*, my play about Mormons running amok and doing things like murdering gay people. But it's all been part of a purposeful plan. Now I'm entering phase two."

According to several Hollywood sources, LaBute never takes a meeting anymore without handing each person a pass-along card. Gwyneth Paltrow, star of LaBute's adaptation of A.S. Byatt's *Possession*, said she collected all seven pass-along cards during the shoot and kept them tucked in the frame of her dressing-room mirror. "They seemed really important to Neil, so I didn't want to throw them away," she said. "I even looked at the website once, but it was kind of—well, it just didn't grab my interest."

"We don't have any big names yet like Cruise or Travolta, but if I keep sharing it, they'll come around."

Despite some resistance, LaBute claims Mormonism will become Hollywood's next Scientology. "It's only a matter of time," he said. "We don't have any big names yet like Cruise or Travolta, but if I keep sharing it, they'll come around. Let's just say one really big name is looking into Mormonism, and it'll be the *pits* if he doesn't convert. I have another celebrity friend reading the Book of Mormon, and I think it's *fostering* a real interest in her."

Asked what lies ahead for him, LaBute said he has entered discussions with the church to write and direct the next Legacy Theater production. "They're giving me free rein to dramatize the Mountain Meadow Massacre any way I see fit," he said.

those skimpy leotards. There will be no temptation of the flesh on our video."

"It's like watching conference, except healthier."

Thornton is certain the video will be a bestseller. "It's like watching conference, except healthier."

Tabercize! Getting Mormons on Their Feet
By Teancum Zenos Smoot IV

SALT LAKE CITY—In an effort to help more Latter-day Saints follow the Word of Wisdom, Salt Lake City–based video company Rock and Roll of My Salvation has released *Tabercize!*, a workout video led by the Mormon Tabernacle Choir.

"We know we have a sizable audience," said Bob Thornton, producer of the workout video. "People are already used to standing up when the choir comes on the television set."

But now, says Thornton, instead of going to the fridge or grabbing another handful of Girl Scout cookies to prepare for the next speaker, the watcher is encouraged to join in exercise routines set to the get-up-and-dance beat of the LDS people's favorite hymns, such as "If You Could Hie to Kolob," "Ye Elders of Israel," and, of course, "God Be With You Till We Meet Again."

The members of the choir will lead the viewer in exercises such as the page turn, the bow, the galumph-to-your-feet, and the hold-that-note head waggle.

"We think the LDS community will appreciate that we've dressed the Tabernacle Choir singers modestly," said Thornton, "unlike most exercise videos on the market, where you can practically see everything through

Keith Richards Objects to Posthumous Baptism
By Molly Thatcher Woodruff

LONDON, ENGLAND—Rolling Stones guitarist Keith Richards is questioning why he has already been baptized for the dead in a Mormon temple. "My publicist has been fielding calls all week," he fumed to an *Enquirer* reporter. "I don't know what they think they're playing at, but as you can see I'm perfectly fine!"

Further investigation revealed that a California youth submitted the name and then performed the baptism during a youth temple trip. "My grandparents fell in love at a Stones concert, and I just wanted to honor them," the young man said. "When I saw a picture of Keith Richards in the paper, I thought it was an obituary."

"I'm like a dirt bike flying in the midst of heaven—varr-rooooom!" said Jensen, riding an imaginary dirt bike.

Church media watchers say they're pleased with all aspects of the article except the section devoted to a polygamous family in Utah that runs its own dirt bike team called "Families Are for Revvin'."

The article features a polygamous Utah family that runs its own dirt bike team called "Families Are for Revvin'."

However, the Relief Society objects to the magazine's use of female models in the Babes, Bikinis 'n' Bikes section. "Those girls are not being true to the Young Women values," said Maureen Dunsmore, second counselor in the general Relief Society presidency.

Several additional magazines are currently planning articles on Mormonism, including *Industrial Carpet, Amalgamated Subway Engineers of America*, and *Packing Peanuts Today*.

Church Featured in *Dirt Bike* Magazine

By Teancum Zenos Smoot IV

URBANA, IL—*Dirt Bike* magazine is featuring the Salt Lake temple on the cover of this month's issue. The article, which gives revealing glimpses into the dirt-biking experiences of some high-profile Mormons, has been lauded by professional and garden-variety dirt bikers alike.

"I didn't know those guys could tear it up like that, dude," said Scott "Handlebar Head" Marks. "Maybe there's something to those Mormons."

Dirk "Gravel Butt" Jensen was similarly impressed, so much so that he applied a sticker to his bike depicting the Angel Moroni, a popular Mormon symbol.

Predictions for the Future

An LDS scientist will invent a urine test to detect levels of spirituality.

Members will be counseled to avoid computer solitaire games, because virtual playing cards are just as bad as real ones.

Their Music Sucks, But It's Appropriate

PROVO, UT—The newest band on the LDS music scene epitomizes its name: Appropriate Train.

Lead singer Dwight Davenport got the idea for the band while listening to his BYU roommate's gangsta rap. "It was horrible," Davenport said. "Some of the words were filthy and disgusting. But there was this one nice part about a kitty cat or something."

Davenport brought together five young men who have made it their life's mission to bring appropriate music to the youth of the church. Borrowing $50,000 from their fathers, all five of whom are currently serving in stake presidencies, they recorded their first CD at Pinnacle Studios in Orem, Utah.

"The spirit of Donny Osmond could be felt all over the place, and that encouraged us," Davenport said.

"The boys sing so sweetly about saying no to coffee and Coke. This is what we'll listen to in the celestial kingdom."

They named their first album *Here Come Da Spirit.* "We produce clean, wholesome music that can evoke the Spirit," the CD booklet states. "Any youth listening exclusively to our music will not only go on a mission but also get married in the temple." Indeed, that claim appears as a guarantee on the CD's back cover: "Mission and temple, or your money back."

"I think their music is great," says Provo housewife LaVerle Rasmussen. "No bad lyrics, no evil guitars or drums, only organ and piano accompaniment. And the boys sing so sweetly about pussycats and saying no to coffee and Coke. This is what we'll listen to in the celestial kingdom."

Ticket sales were slow for Appropriate Train's debut concert at BYU's Marriott Center until the Religion Department offered extra-credit in all religion classes. However, one of the songs had to be removed from the program. "There's something about that pussycat song," an administrator complained. "I can't place my finger on it, but it doesn't seem appropriate."

Predictions for the Future

A gang called the Gadianton Robbers will terrorize Utah County.

A J. Golden Kimball anecdote involving the F-word will surface.

The Church will extend the priesthood to every worthy male Democrat.

Thousands Attend Nordstrom Open House and Dedication

By Jack B. Kimball

OREM, UT—In twelve sessions attended by more than 20,000 people, Nordstrom chief executive officer Jeffrey Hancock dedicated a new Nordstrom department store in Orem last week. Having long been forced to drive forty miles north to the Nordstrom at Fashion Place Mall in Murray, Utah County residents are rejoicing to finally have this upscale department store in their midst.

"I'm grateful to live in a day when blessings are filling the land," said area woman Kate Greenshaw. "I thank heaven for Novell, Nu Skin, and all the high-tech companies who've lifted this county to a new level. The blessings of heaven have poured down upon our valley."

With tears in her eyes, another woman said: "I always said I would go to Nordstrom more often if one was closer to me. Now I can."

During the traditional celebratory shout, Nordstrom patrons waved colorful silk Hermés scarves.

Attended only by those who met stringent credit requirements, the dedicatory sessions concluded with Nordstrom's traditional celebratory shout. Before the event, Nordstrom outlets throughout the West shipped thousands of silk Hermés scarves to Orem for patrons to purchase and wave during the shout.

Prior to the dedication, more than 80,000 people toured the building during a public open house. "The beauty of the building and the spirit of the occasion really touched some hearts," reported store manager Joseph Anderson. "About eight hundred people opened Nordstrom charge accounts on the spot, and thousands more took home the mail-in application."

A Nordstrom spokeswoman confirmed that the company is considering opening smaller outlets in areas where the population isn't sufficient to support a full-scale store. "We've already purchased land for a prototype in Parowan," said Amelia Cobain. "The smaller stores will be one level and have less square footage. Some of the usual amenities will not be included, such as aquariums, an in-house café, and a clothing alteration service. Local shoppers will need to take responsibility for their own clothing alterations."

Couple Finds *Erin Brockovich* "Really Good" Despite R-Rating
By Lisa Layton

MODESTO, CA—Jane Doe, a devoted Julia Roberts fan who spoke on condition of anonymity, admitted that she and her husband John watched *Erin Brockovich* on video after succumbing to arguments that "it was actually really uplifting." Furthermore, Doe stated, she and her husband enjoyed the movie and found it "really good" despite its R-rating.

"My sister is inactive and she sees whatever she wants, and she's been nagging and taunting me for ages," Doe stated. "When we were talking about movies one day, she said, 'Oh, I forgot, you didn't see *Erin Brockovich*, even though it's Julia's best movie ever.' That drove me crazy, let me tell you, because I've loved Julia Roberts ever since *Mystic Pizza*."

Doe said she had not been planning to rent *Erin Brockovich* at the video store that day. "I was just going to get some more stuff for the kids, but the store had this special, five movies for five days for five dollars. I got *Chicken Run* and a couple other cartoons, and then I just saw it there, like it was waiting for me. I didn't see anyone I knew in the store,

so I just rented it. I was worried about how John would respond, let me tell you, but he said he was willing to watch it with me after all."

"And wouldn't you know, my sister was completely right," Doe said. "I mean, I got sick of all the profanity, and every time someone swore I would say a little prayer. But still, when it was all over, I felt inspired and uplifted, glad to know there are devoted, hardworking, good-hearted people in the world."

"Every time someone swore, I would say a little prayer."

Despite her enjoyment of the movie, Doe said she would not be recommending it to anyone else. "Are you kidding? Are you forgetting I'm not using my real name? The movie police in our ward are fierce. My visiting teachers freaked out when they saw John's copies of *Terminator* and *The Jerk*, which he bought in high school. Now he keeps them in the garden shed."

Mormon Community Awards

First member of the Cedar Ridge [Utah] Ward Relief Society to read past 2 Nephi: Laura Palmatier

Following the lesson manual to a T all year long: Mary Diarte, Aberdeen, WA

Review of Spider-Man
By LeVoy Mann

I always help my family members and coworkers evaluate entertainment choices by asking them to consider questions like these: Does it make me feel worthy to kneel in prayer? Are the values being portrayed virtuous, lovely, of good report, or praiseworthy? (See A of F 1:13.) Are my entertainment choices bringing me closer to heaven? Is this taking me away from more important things I should be doing?

After evaluating these questions, I decided it would be best to see the new *Spider-Man* movie as soon as possible, so I could alert those I love if there was anything offensive. And believe me, there was.

The movie opens with Peter Parker explaining that the entire story is based on his lust for a girl. This particular girl is Mary Jane Watson, a neighbor of his since the age of four, a girl so devoid of the Young Women values that she feels she must parade her curvy hypnotic form to the world through her bedroom window. With young Peter's window a mere twenty feet from hers, it's no wonder he can't keep his obviously intelligent mind focused on his family and schoolwork.

After being bitten by a genetically enhanced spider, Peter discovers he has new powers, like increased strength and miniscule hairs on his extremities. Most disconcerting of all, a sticky web-like gel keeps spurting from him. The obvious parallel with hormone-ridden puberty changes are obvious, and it was all I could do to keep from running from the theater while he "experimented" with his new body.

The one truly moral character is Parker's uncle, who tries to teach his nephew that "with great power comes great responsibility." I thought of the priesthood and how some abuse that great privilege while others responsibly use it to aid others and maintain order. To my horror, the uncle was killed off early in the movie, leaving Parker in the questionable hands of his Aunt May. This woman prays in a completely inappropriate manner and even encourages mission-age Peter to pursue Mary Jane instead of putting in his papers.

Most disconcerting of all, a sticky web-like gel keeps spurting from the main character.

This courtship eventually leads into the most offensive scene in the movie. During a rainstorm, the costumed actor playing Spider-Man is suspended upside-down while French-kissing the inappropriately dressed Mary Jane in public. I buried my nose in my popcorn bag, paying no attention to the wet T-shirt of that handmaid in Zion and the straining, veined neck of the web-man. I just hope none of my fellow brethren in the priesthood saw me in that darkened theater, counting the seconds to when this travesty would end.

I give this movie one star out of four for a few well-acted scenes of dialogue between Willem Dafoe and his son. But, be warned: throughout the feature, I was bombarded with scenes of violence, vengeance, and mayhem. People were roughly shoved into walls, thrown through windows, and dropped from great heights. Property-damaging explosions provided the backdrop for immoral behavior and worldly wrestlers. It will take a lot of editing for CleanFlicks to make this video appropriate for my household.

Log Flume Ride Announced for Nauvoo

By Jack B. Kimball

NAUVOO, ILLINOIS—With the rebuilt Nauvoo temple now gracing this small Illinois town where Mormonism once thrived, the church has stirred up new excitement by announcing that a log-flume ride will be built adjacent to the Heber C. Kimball home.

"Nauvoo is the church's premiere historical site and one of our most important tourist attractions, second only to Temple Square itself," said Elder J. Tuttle Erickson. "With all the exhibits and drama productions we already put on here, it makes sense to think more in terms of a real theme park. We're not talking about something crass like Disneyland, but something tasteful and historically complementary. I don't know of anything that says 'pioneer frontier' like a log flume ride."

To help establish the ride's historical value, timber for the structure will be taken from nearby forests where early Mormon pioneers procured wood for their homes. "Of course, we'll also use the distinctive red Nauvoo brick," Elder Tuttle said. "The ride will be manned by senior missionaries dressed in period costume, and they'll share the gospel with people waiting in line."

Elder Tuttle explained that because the new temple is open only to faithful Saints, leaders felt it would help maintain a balance in Nauvoo to build another facility that everyone can enjoy. "If we can't warm their bosoms with inspiration, at least we'll tickle their tummies with a fun ride," Elder Tuttle said.

"If we can't warm their bosoms with inspiration, at least we'll tickle their tummies with a fun ride."

Future plans include a monorail connecting the temple, the visitors' center, and Joseph Smith's Mansion House. "To boost visitors in the off-season," Elder Tuttle said, "we're considering an annual Nauvoo Halloween festival, with pumpkin patches and spook alleys and everything."

Mormon Community Awards

Resisting the temptation to reverse the yeses and nos while singing "Shall the Youth of Zion Falter": Corey Sherwin, Bountiful, UT

Most Modest Swimsuit: Taylor Gardner, Anaheim, CA

"I quit Dr. Pepper once in 1981 when my daughter was born, but that only lasted about a week," commented Paige Christiansen of Orem, Utah. "I quit in 1992 for two weeks using a caffeinated gum. I've probably quit a thousand times in between, but I've never made it more than 24 hours. I never hear the still, small voice in my head, and I'm sure caffeine is the reason why not. I can't wait to get the spirit back!"

New Caffeine Patch Announced
By LeVoy Mann

OGDEN, UT—Help may be just around the corner for the estimated one million Mormons addicted to caffeine. Robinson Consumer Products has announced that Caff-trol®, the first caffeine patch cleared for sale to consumers without a physician's prescription, is now available throughout the Intermountain West in pharmacies, supermarkets, and other outlets.

"It's a great day for sinners who are ready to begin taking control of their caffeine habits," said LeBryant Perkins, Robinson Consumer Products president. "Caffeine drinkers now have a proven tool to help them quit this filthy and disgusting addiction."

"Caffeine drinkers now have a proven tool to help them quit this filthy and disgusting addiction."

A 15-mg Caff-trol® patch is worn each day for six weeks. Starter kits include a week's supply of seven patches and the Caff-trol® Pathways to Change® behavioral support system, which features the *Taking Action* booklet and an audiotape designed to help consumers deal with the psychological stresses of quitting. Refill kits include a one-week supply of seven 15-mg patches and a booklet titled *Staying the Course*.

Greg Olsen Enters "Blue Period"

By Teancum Zenos Smoot IV

PROVO, UT—The death of the Olsen family dog, Ralphy, has plunged popular LDS artist Greg Olsen into what future art critics will no doubt call his "blue period."

"When Ralphy was . . . brought home, I knew that my art would change forever," Olsen said as he slumped in a chair at the Cougar Eat in BYU's Wilkenson Student Center, chain-drinking cups of hot cocoa.

Olsen's work has changed subtly since Ralphy's death, incorporating considerably more shades of blue than is usual for the artist. In addition, he is painting in a more modernist style, shunning the verisimilitude that has marked most of his work. For example, *The Old Guitarist* depicts, with heart-rending emotion, the inner fears and dark broodings of a man playing a special musical number on his guitar during sacrament meeting.

Many are calling *Little Kid Interrupts Family Prayer* Olsen's most challenging, provocative work ever.

Blue Nude in a One-Piece Bathing Suit

Other pieces representative of Olsen's newer work include *Blue Nude in a One-Piece Bathing Suit* and *Little Kid Interrupts Family Prayer*, which many are calling his most challenging, provocative work ever. Citing disapproval of the Correlation Committee, the *Ensign* magazine has declined to run all three new pieces.

Thomas Kincaid, the famous "painter of light," said he sympathizes with Olsen. "I went through a similar period when I was known by a select few as 'the painter of darkness,'" Kincaid said. "Man, you should've seen that stuff. But allow me to let you in on a trade secret: dark don't sell." Kincaid said

he didn't think blue would fare much better.

However, Olsen, being dedicated to the cause of art, said he would take his chances. "I know my blue period may be pegged as self-referential and overtly sentimental a hundred years from now. People may pine for my return to the vibrant primary colors of my earlier work, and sales may fall off. But I just gotta express myself."

Olsen said he does not expect his blue period to last indefinitely. "I suppose things may look a little rosier later on," he said.

Members Urged to Store a Year's Supply of Entertainment

By Jack B. Kimball

OGDEN, UT—Speaking at a regional fireside last Sunday, Elder Douglas Slaymaker called upon Latter-day Saints everywhere to store a year's supply of CDs, DVDs, videogames, best-selling novels, and other sources of entertainment.

"I'll tell you what, when disaster strikes, the last thing you want is a bunch of hungry, dirty people who are bored out of their minds," said Elder Slaymaker. "Just as our bodies need food, our brains need something to chew on."

Slaymaker said that members should determine each family member's media needs for one year. "When civilization breaks down, you'll want the comfort of essential things like *Princess Bride, Home Alone,* and *Field of Dreams,*" he said. "They're like the wheat in your food storage. But you'll also need the novelty of new things to watch and read. Whenever you buy a new media item, squirrel it away for a year and then rotate it into your media diet. Yes, you'll be a year behind the curve, but that'll help you stay less worldly."

> **"When disaster strikes, the last thing you want is a bunch of hungry, dirty people who are bored out of their minds."**

To power entertainment devices during a civilization collapse, Elder Slaymaker said that a generator would be optimal but that members should also store a year's supply of batteries suitable for portable devices. In addition, he noted that CDs, DVDs, books, games, and other items will provide excellent bartering opportunities in post-civilized society. "I could see a well-worn video of *Princess Bride* going for a whole bushel of wheat. A complete set of *Work and the Glory* novels could probably be traded for several weeks' worth of food. Make sure you store plenty of those LDS romance novels to keep the females warm and hopeful."

Elder Slaymaker concluded by saying, "Brothers and sisters, now is the day of preparation. Watch for sales, and buy an extra media item each time you go to the store. If something bad happens, you won't want to sit around twiddling your thumbs until the trucks roll in from Welfare Square and the insurance inspectors show up. After all, heaven can only help us if we help ourselves."

Biography of Biographer of Famous Mormon Biographer Due Out Soon

By Teancum Zenos Smoot IV

SALT LAKE CITY—In a publication event many Mormon literati are calling "long overdue" and "highly anticipated," Signature Books is releasing the first edition of M. Daniel Quill's biography of the celebrated Mormon biographer Strauss Petersen, who penned the seminal biography of Martina Brooks, famous biographer of B.H. Roberts, author of Joseph Smith's history. The book will be released in August.

Review of Attack of the Clones
By LeVoy Mann

If the *Enquirer* had not hired me as a regular entertainment reviewer, I would not have stood in line for three long days to see this installment of the Star Wars franchise. However, I felt it necessary to see it as soon as possible in order to effectively guide my flock to other pastures, if necessary.

Please, my flock. Seek other entertainment pastures than this travesty of unabashed lust and standards-crushing violence.

In this Star Wars movie, there is a bare female posterior covered only by veil-type netting. The well-proportioned Natalie Portman did not seem ashamed to be seen in some of her outfits and even rolled around in the grass with Hayden Christensen wearing one of them. And I noticed it is she who loses the most clothing in battle (see *1 Tim. 2:9, Gal. 5:19*). If you look closely at the midriff-baring outfit, you can make out her woman-buds and will spend the evening, like me, trying to wrest that image from your mind.

If I met George Lucas, I would shake him firmly and demand the return of loveable characters like the industrious Ewoks.

The concentration of testimony-withering behavior in this film, however, is in violence. There are many human deaths, senseless murders of mechanisms both seen and unseen, and much sci-fi action violence. A boy's father is beheaded by a "light saber," and his son later picks up his father's severed,

helmeted head. A great deal of time is spent on animal attacks of humans and other personified characters. One of the personified characters is consumed by one of the beasts.

A few more important details to warn you about. I have always enjoyed the persona of Yoda, a master of self-control and dignity. In one of the least celestial scenes of the entire saga, this creature engages in a violent duel with another man. Why, George Lucas? Can't you let one character resolve his differences with warm discussions and brotherly love? And is anyone else bothered by the fact that the main character comes from the planet Tatooine, which not only conjures up images of body-defiling tattoos but also the coarse slang term *weener*? What if some impressionable adolescent decides to combine these two elements in one atrocious act?

If I met George Lucas, I would shake him firmly and demand the return of loveable characters like the industrious Ewoks and teach him the plan of happiness. Had I met Luke Skywalker early in his life, I would have testified as to the importance of genealogy. It would have cleared up his confusion and helped him understand his role here on the earth. Or on that planet he comes from.

TV Section: What's on the Mo Channel?

	Monday	Tuesday	Wednesday	Thursday	Friday	Saturday	Sunday
8:00	$25,000 Pyramid Scheme	Cedar Hills 84602	Family Fewd: The Evils of Birth Control	My Favorite Polygamist	My Funny Underwear	Mormon Cooking Marathon / Gordon Bleu Zucchini	General Conference Return Marathon This Week: 1968-72
8:30	All My Wives		Oh My Heck!			Emeril Cooks with Sugar Beets	
9:00	Food Storage Follies	Heber City Five-O	America's Funniest Home Evening Lessons	Orson Scott Card Presents: Tales of the Unacceptable	Smart Guy-CANCELLED because intellectuals are one of the three biggest threats to the church		
9:30	Are You Being Fellowshipped?					Hotplate Cooking for Two Men on $3/75 a Month	
10:00	Donny & Marie Show	Honey, I Shrunk My Paycheck	My Three Sons of Perdition	Mahonri Moriancumer, P.I.	Translated Like Me		
10:30		By Getting a Job in Utah	The Hemline Detectives	Movie: Seven Brides for One Brother	Touched By a Walker Texas		
11:00	The Flying Sister Missionary	I Dream of Jeannie and Laura and Lynette and Monique and Betty and…			Providence	Julia Child's Jell-O Dishes	
11:30							
12:00	Candid Camera, Girls Camp Edition	Carthage Justice	My So-Called Herbalife	Who Wants to Pay a Million Dollars in Tithing?		Yanni Can Can	
12:30			Disgusting Things Deacons Do				
1:00	I Love Lucy at Arm's Length	I Married an R.M.		The Young and the Restless During Sacrament Meeting	Straight Eye for an R.M. Guy	Donner Party Fixin's	
1:30		I Was a Teenaged Scoutmaster					
2:00	Little House on the Prairie	J. Golden Kimball Says the Darnedest Things	Mandi Meecham, Fashion Police Girl		Six Feet Under the Waters of Baptism	This Old Fundamentalist Compound	
2:30							
3:00	Mighty Mormon Power Rangers	Mighty Mormon Power Rangers	Mighty Mormon Power Rangers	Mighty Mormon Power Rangers	Mighty Mormon Power Rangers		
3:30							
4:00	Powerpuff Sisters	Powerpuff Sisters	Powerpuff Sisters	Powerpuff Sisters	Powerpuff Sisters	The Bill Cosby Show	
4:30	Sponge Bob Black Tag	Sponge Bob Black Tag	Sponge Bob Black Tag	Sponge Bob Black Tag	Sponge Bob Black Tag		
5:00	Babylon Hive	Kimball's Creek	One Simple Rule for Dating My Teenage Daughter	That '50s Show	The Uplifting Report	My Three Nephites	
5:30							
6:00	Dr. Quinn: Mormon Historian	Law & Order: Honor Code Unit	Really Full House	Survivor: BYU	Saint Trek: The Next Generation	Saturday Night Appropriate	
6:30							
7:00	Movies with Ebert and Dutcher	Chastity and the City	Resisting Temptation Island	Muffy, the Anti-Mormon Slayer	West Wing C.O.B.	The Late, Late, Late Show	
7:30				Movie: My Big Fat Temple Wedding			
8:00	Movie: Princess Bride	Missionaries Behaving Badly	Movie: Stake Basketball Diaries		Movie: Prepubescent Bride	Movie: Monty Python's Search for the Holy Grail (Edited)	
8:30							
9:00	Movie: Mister Hatch Goes To Washington				Provo Baywatch	Why Are You Wasting Time Watching TV When You Could Be Reading the Scriptures, Doing Your Home Teaching, or Researching Your Genealogy?	
9:30							
10:00	General Authority Squares		The Osmonds/Osbournes Deathmatch 2003				
10:30	General Conference Bloopers and Practical Jokes	Most Embarrassing Testimonies Caught on Tape	NuSkin Pay Per View				
11:00			BYUPD Blue	This Is Your Pre-Mortal Life	This Is the Place!		

"Best Loved" Series Goes Yiddish

By Teancum Zenos Smoot IV

SALT LAKE CITY—Following in the tradition of *Best Loved Stories of the LDS People* and *Best Loved Poetry of the LDS People*, Deseret Book has announced that it will soon release the first CD in the Best Loved series, titled *Best Loved Traditional Yiddish Folksongs of the LDS People*. The CD will include such genuine, rustic Yiddish tunes as "Matchmaker, Matchmaker," "If I Were a Rich Man," and "Sunrise, Sunset."

High Hopes for Pride Cycle Shop Dashed

By Terrill W. Cannon

CENTERVILLE, UT—Davis County newcomer Joel Harris will close his new bicycle shop after being open for only a month. Harris, a Methodist, has no explanation for the "absolute lack" of patronage he's received.

When preparing the shop and hanging the Pride Cycle Shop sign, he received plenty of attention. "People would slow down and take a good long look," Harris says. "But when I held the grand opening, the place was a ghost town. I guess Mormon people just don't like bikes."

Snapshot

What are we naming our Mormon punk bands?

Murmur

Laban's Head

Inappropriate

Outer Darkness

Past Feeling

Secret Combination

Ripened in Iniquity

Sons of Perdition

Lone and Dreary World

The Gadianton Band

Double-Pierced

Extermination Order

The Less Active

Cipher in the Snow

Stiff-Necked

Predictions for the Future

The Miracle of Forgiveness will be required reading for 6.7 percent more teenagers this year than last year.

Gerald Lund will announce plans for a new five-volume historical fiction series set during the presidency of Howard W. Hunter.

Snapshot

What positions are we trying from the newly published Mormon Kama Sutra?

Retention and Reactivation

The Stripling Warrior

Urim and Thummim

I Have Two Little Hands

The Second Coming

Hie to Kolob

The PPI

I'll Go Where You Want Me to Go

"Give," Said the Little Stream

The Burning Bush

A Banner Is Unfurled

The Secret Combination

Head, Shoulders, Knees, and Toes

Come, Thou Font of Every Blessing

Hold to the Rod

The Rameumptom

Predictions for the Future

A multilevel-marketing company in Utah will discover, bottle, and market an exotic fruit drink that erases sin and increases spirituality.

Terry Tempest Williams Caught with Strange Desert

By Teancum Zenos Smoot IV

CASTLE VALLEY, UT—Only months after the publication of Mormon author Terry Tempest Williams's new book celebrating her "erotic" relationship with Utah's deserts, Williams was caught in a compromising position with Mongolia's Gobi Desert.

Two backpackers reported seeing Williams sensuously running her fingers through the Gobi Desert's sand and rapturously embracing large rocks. Further investigation turned up some lipstick marks on native wildlife in the area.

News of Williams's affair with a desert on the other side of the planet has affected the usually upbeat nature of Utah's deserts. Bob Silas, a ranger in the Goblin Valley area, reported that the giant joshuas seem much droopier since Williams's indiscretion was revealed. "And I swear I've been seeing Edward Abbey's ghost peeking in through the camper windows," Seeger said. "I had to throw my copy of *Refuge* out the window to get rid of him."

Many of Williams's human fans expressed shock at the scandal. "The relationship Terry had with the Utah deserts in *Desert Quartet* was so beautiful," wept Muriel Southby. "What made her wander like this?"

Chapter 9:
Words of Wisdom

Mormons believe that every individual is given certain spiritual gifts. Some men are exceptionally adept at picking neckties that don't clash with their white shirts. Some women are unparalleled at making tuna casseroles with potato chips crumbled on top. Some adult Mormons even possess the uncanny ability to teach the thirteen-year-olds in Sunday school week after week without suffering a nervous breakdown—at least, nothing so bad that Prozac can't smooth it over.

Occasionally, however, you'll meet a Mormon whose spiritual gifts run deeper than normal. At the *Enquirer*, we pride ourselves on providing a forum for Mormonism's only widely published bona-fide psychic, a good brother named Mahonri who helps folks with all kinds of problems. Perhaps even more remarkably, twelve-year-old Mandi Meecham has established a devoted worldwide following through her *Enquirer* advice column. And those are only two of our most popular, prolific, prophetic writers.

Everyone can glean something worthwhile from this chapter's counsel and inspiration, whether you get a stupor of thought or a burning in the bosom. You'll get more out of this chapter if you fast for twenty-four hours before reading it. But remember, this book shouldn't become a replacement for your own prayers and scripture study!

Ask a Beehive

By Mandi Meecham,
age 12
Draper 34th Ward,
Draper Utah
Southeast Stake

Question: I have a coworker who is anti-Mormon, and he says the church is polytheistic because a prophet once claimed that Adam is actually God. What would be an effective way to defend Mormonism from this claim?
—James P. Solomon, systems analyst

Answer: Anti-Mormons are just so lame and creepy. I saw some outside Temple Square and this one guy had yellow teeth. Hello! Get a dental plan! And this other guy with major halitosis was screaming something about how Mormons aren't Christians and his hair was all dredded out and I was like, "Hi, let me help you, that look is way too old-school for words." Those dudes are totally going to be soooo sorry when they get booted on down to Utter Darkness. How sweet will THAT be!

Prophets have probably said a whole bunch of things, and maybe people were like, whoa, whatever. Prophets speak all weird sometimes. And most of them lived way long ago and probably spoke some kind of old-people English, which sounds totally dope but is way hard to get. Like Shakespeare, who is way ancient and said things like "Hey, you fellow country men, lend your ears to me." That is whacked! So maybe this prophet was all, "Hey, Adam is an archangel," but nobody got it. Like the way I totally don't get Shakespeare. If that brainiac Liz DeCapra wasn't in my class, I'd be tanking it. She is the bomb.

Question: My husband and I have always had a happy marriage, but it seems like lately he spends more time at work and less time with our two daughters and me. We haven't been to the temple in almost a year, because he's always at work. What can I do?

—Lavara Bennion, scrapbook consultant

Answer: Um, HELLO all you lame dads who work all the time! Here's a quarter so you can buy a life! Anyway, you should just tell him, "Duh, come home sometimes. No success at work can accommodate for failure to be at home." I learned that one in Sunday School last week because we were doing this way tedious stupid hangman game because Brother and Sister Vale were all "Sorry, but we're sort of unprepared" and stuff. Whatever.

Prophets have probably said a whole bunch of things, and maybe people were like, whoa, whatever.

So they put that whole saying on the board and were like "That will take you forever!" but Connor Metten got it right away because he stole their notes when they weren't looking, and then the Vales were all bummed because they didn't know what to do with us next, and they were all "Let's just read some scriptures." Then Kallie Simmons poked me and was like "Dude, I'm OUT of here" and I pretended we had girl issues and had to go to the bathroom but we snuck out instead and scored free donuts at Krispy Kreme because the guy there is hot for Kallie. Dude, that was RICH.

Mahonri the Mormon Psychic

Dear Mahonri: The wheat tins in my basement say they're from 1972. I'm worried the wheat may be too old to keep. But we spent so much money on it, and I don't want to spend more to replace it. Should I discard it, or will it keep until the Millennium? Enclosed are a few sample kernels.
—Rotation-Challenged in Rotorua

Dear Rotation-Challenged: I placed your sample kernels into one of my great-grandmother's heirloom canning jars and prayed and pondered over them. I'm afraid the kernels blew up in a poof of green smoke, leaving behind a residue resembling mold spores. If you don't get rid of the old wheat now, it will soon turn toxic and cost you thousands in cleanup. And your insurance won't cover it!

Dear Mahonri: I think our food storage room is cursed. It started a few weeks ago when a jar of peaches fell off the shelf in the middle of the night. A month ago, a brown recluse spider bit my husband while he was looking for the camp stove. Just yesterday, a package of toilet paper somehow got too near an exposed light bulb and almost burned down the house. I'm scared to find out what's next! Can you help us?
—Panicky in Panguitch

Dear Panicky: Brace yourself, because I have some bad news. For this problem, I consulted my crystal ball. I'm afraid I witnessed your teenage son using the food storage room as a place to read inappropriate magazines. The food storage room is the spiritual heart of any good Mormon home, and your son's desecration of that sacred space explains the disruptions. You need to reprove him with sharpness and then show forth an increase in love. Also, hang some Mormon-Ads in the food storage room to dispel the bad vibes and discourage further misuse. And change the doorknob to a non-locking variety.

Dear Mahonri: My 11-year-old daughter likes to eat Jell-O straight out of the box. She shakes the powder into her mouth and just lets it melt! I've tried hiding our supply, but she always finds it, almost as if she can sense sugar vibes (maybe she has a psychic gift too). Our dentist bills are skyrocketing, and I'm concerned about her health. Is this just a phase, or do I need to take drastic action?
—Jittery in Bountiful, Utah

A tarot reading tells me that what Jell-O is to your daughter now, drugs will become in her future.

Dear Jittery: A tarot reading tells me that what Jell-O is to your daughter now, drugs will become in her future, unless you act immediately to break her cycle of abuse. However, weaning her will be hard. If you get rid of your Jell-O altogether, she will simply steal it from other people's food storage. You must create a trap for her by replacing half the contents of a Jell-O box with citric-acid powder. The sour shock will probably cure her, but keep putting her on the prayer roll till she goes a full month clean.

Ask a Young Mother
By Sue Bergin
Sugarhouse 32nd
Ward, Sugarhouse
Utah North Stake

Question: My fiancé really likes kissing—a lot! I enjoy kissing too, but I'm afraid that if we kiss too much, we'll be tempted to try other things as well, and I really want to stay morally clean and have a temple wedding. He keeps pressuring me for longer and longer kisses. What do you think I should tell him?

Answer: Actually, kissing is a lovely— McKay, dear, no no no no. The turtle does not like to live in the toilet. Kissing is a lovely and tender way to express—honey, no. Put Turtle back in his cage now or no mac and cheese for dinner—kissing expresses your— MOMMY SAID NO. NO NAIL POLISH ON THE TURTLE. Put it back. NOW. No, he doesn't like faces painted on his shell. No.

Anyway, I think kissing can be a good thing if it's kept gentle and holy and if you don't—Kelsey, take the nail polish from McKay. No, the nail polish. The nail polish. THE NAIL POLISH. No, TAKE it. TAKE it from him. Don't give him more. NO, TAKE IT AWAY FROM HIM. Thank you—if you don't use any tongue.

Basically, kissing is holy if you—Kelsey, just take the polish. Don't hit. We don't hit. McKay, honey, Kelsey is sorry. Stop crying or you'll wake the baby. Stop. Kelsey, say you're sorry. Say you're sorry. KELSEY, come back with Mommy's mascara. Mommy's mascara goes back. Put it back. PUT IT BACK. No, on the shelf. No, just give it to me. To me. TO ME. Thank you—it's holy if you only kiss chastely, with closed mouths and with lots

of—McKay, no no no. Don't go visit baby. Baby's sleeping. Baby doesn't want you to play her a song on your flute. No, McKay. No. MCKAY, DON'T OPEN THAT DOOR!— with lots of lights on.

It's holy if you only kiss chastely, with closed mouths and with lots of—McKay, no no no.

Don't go somewhere dark where you'll— Kelsey, could you close Baby's door? Kelsey? Please close the door. Please get McKay out of Baby's room. Kelsey? Get McKay out of Kylee's room. Out. No, out. OUT. Close the door—never mind. Yes, McKay, baby is crying now. Mommy will get her up. Anyway, don't go somewhere dark or you'll be tempted to be unchaste.

Poet's Corner

Patriarchal Ardor

I see you across the Gospel Doctrine class,
Taupe Dockers pressed with razor-sharp
*   pleat*
(piercing my eternal soul)

O feel the burning in my bosom
For I know (beyond a shadow of doubt)
*   that your love is true*
Fellowship me, indoctrinate me,
Correlate me

My stomach soars and flips like a giddy
*   Sunbeam class*
No second witness need testify of this truth:
You are the stake president of my heart

Ask a Beehive
By Mandi Meecham,
age 12
Draper 34th Ward,
Draper Utah
Southeast Stake

Question: A friend of mine recently asked me why it took so long for the church to extend the priesthood to all worthy members. It seems that in the early days, blacks were given the priesthood, but at some point I guess it stopped. I've read the official declaration of 1978, which ended the discriminatory practice, but I can't seem to find an official declaration that started it. Can you help me?

—Gil Sanderson, networking specialist

Answer: Black people are so hip. They totally add diversity, and that is soooo good because they can expand your mind and teach you things that white people just don't get. I saw this black guy—they like to be called "Afro-Americans"—last Saturday when Lindsay and I were at the Gateway. Lindsay stopped at the Ear Piercery because she really wants to pierce her ears up on top even though her dad would kill her.

So she was all tripping for these silver goldfish earrings and I was staring into that puke factory Chik-Fil-A, and there was this black guy standing there. DUDE, black guys even make standing in line look good. He was a tall yummy drink of HOT cocoa. This guy was wearing distressed B.U.M. jeans that would look so stupid on the guys in my school. I was like, "Lindsay, check the eye candy over there. Doesn't he go to Alta?" and she was all, "Mand, hello . . . you're only into blonde guys who snowboard," and SHE rolled her eyes.

She is four months younger than me, and so of course she doesn't understand how my tastes have matured.

Then I had this epitome about the whole thing, which I learned about in English class—it's this thing where you learn something about yourself. I realized that Lindsay was sort of, like, oppressing me because she was trying to tell me who to like and who not to like. Then I had this massive head rush and thought, dude, this black guy has been oppressed and stuff too because of slavery and Martin Luther King and all that, so we are practically soul mates. And he obviously knows much more than the other feebs my age.

I felt this total connection to him and wondered if we hung out in the pre-existence.

I felt this total connection to him and wondered if we hung out in the pre-existence. But before I could go say anything to him, he grabbed his fries and left, and I was way bummed. But if it is meant to be, then I'll totally see him again and we'll know it by looking into each other's eyes. That's how it works. So, anyway, maybe blacks didn't have the priesthood before because it was like, "Guys, you are way cool already, and I gave you this slammin' fashion sense, so stop complaining."

Mahonri the Mormon Psychic

Dear Mahonri: We're having a weird situation related to our bedroom fan, which we sleep with every night for improved air circulation. Whenever we go to bed past midnight, the fan starts making a strange noise as soon as we turn out the lights. It's an almost human-sounding voice saying something like "ooooohm-eeeeeeeeee." We can't shake the sensation that something more is going on here than just a mechanical problem. We've enclosed a dust sample from the fan. Can you help?

—Puzzled and a Little Spooked in Magna

Dear Puzzled: Thank you for enclosing the specimen of dust from the fan blade—that kind of thing can be very useful. After applying several of my exclusive diagnostic techniques to the dust, I determined the need to hold what I call a one-man séance. It took three sessions, but I was finally able to make contact with your recently departed Uncle Carl, who is currently languishing in what amounts to a halfway house in the spirit world. Your uncle is warning you not to make the same mistake he did. What he has been trying to communicate to you through the medium of the fan is simply this: "Do your home teaching."

Dear Mahonri: I feel a little sheepish writing you, because I don't really have a problem I can put my finger on. We just moved into a beautiful new home, but somehow it feels spiritually flat. My husband has become crabbier, and our teenage son and daughter have seemed more withdrawn and worldly. As for me, I haven't

been getting the same joy out of my scrapbooking. Are those enough details for you to analyze our vibe and give some suggestions?

—In the Doldrums in Dana Point

Dear Doldrums: I meditated over your letter while burning a stick of my best incense, and in time I was able to summon images of your household in my crystal ball. Sister, here is your problem: you have the Mormon equivalent of a feng shui imbalance. The Chinese are concerned with the proper flow of ch'i, or energy, through their households; Mormons, on the other hand, are concerned with the flow of inspiration.

Here is your problem: you have the Mormon equivalent of a feng shui imbalance.

I see several places in your house where you need to rearrange your furnishings and décor to maximize right angles and square patterns—particularly in your living room, where the furniture is all diagonally oriented and the drapes are a little too poofy. Another thing that will help is hanging a framed photo of the temple in your entryway instead of that scribbly-looking art thing. Also, I recommend the music of Michael McLean instead of that jangly stuff. And tell your husband and son that leaving up the toilet lid interferes with a household's spiritual flow—that's a lesson I learned a long time ago.

Mormon Sports with "Iron" Rod Zeier

Question: Just once, I'd like to hear a sports commentator respond to this: How can you justify the huge salaries professional athletes make, when teachers and nurses and police officers are so badly underpaid? How can you defend those salaries?

—Shelly from Bountiful

Dear Shelly: Hey, we get this one all the time, and all your question says to me is that you haven't studied the issue very carefully. Let's think about it a sec, okay? Where do athletes get their money? They get it from the teams they play for. And where do those teams get it? They get it from television, mostly. And where does television get it? From advertising. And what is the main product advertised during sporting events on television? Beer. So professional athletes get their money from beer companies.

So who do you think should have all that money? Evil beer companies? Breweries? People who knowingly use sexy models to sell a dangerous, addictive, but legal substance? Is that who you think should have all the money? Or should professional athletes? Don't talk to me about nurses or teachers, most of whom don't even drink beer much because they can't afford it. We're talking about the money here, and it's money that would go one of two places: to athletes or to beer companies. So who is morally better? Talented, hard-working young men who inspire us all with how fast they can run and

jump and do things with their various balls that just take your breath away? Or fat old brewery owners?

Already you can see how rich athletes are not the problem you're making them out to be. But let's look at the problem a little deeper. What happens to the money after athletes get it? You know the answer as well as I do: they spend it. That money trickles down into society, to Lexus dealers and honest jewelers and bail bondsmen and stripper club bouncers, like my cousin Lennie, who, you know, may be a few french-fries shy of a Happy Meal but who is an honest, hard-working shmoe who deserves a few extra benjamins at the end of the day. Also, these athletes pay taxes, and that's not all. Look at all the LDS professional athletes, your John Taits, your Shawn Bradleys, your Brandon Domans. Look at the extra tithing they're able to pay. So who do you think should have the money, Shelly? Beer companies, or the church? And then talk to me about overpaid athletes.

Look at all the LDS professional athletes. Look at the extra tithing they're able to pay.

Props to the peeps, and remember, you can catch "Iron" Rod on *Mormon Sports*, mornings eight to noon on KMOR. Rest of you homies, peace, and we'll catch you on the rebound.

Ask a Beehive

By Mandi Meecham,
age 12
Draper 34th Ward,
Draper Utah
Southeast Stake

Question: Lately I've been having trouble sleeping at night because of all the unrest in the Middle East. I don't understand why the Arab-Israeli conflict has gone on so long and what can be done about it. How, as Mormons, should we react to this conflict? What can we do to help?
—Karen Hull, stay-at-home mother

Answer: OK, I TOTALLY can answer this question because one of my favorite movies talks about this conflict and it is way deep and made me go, like, whoa, jump back. Brendan Fraser in *The Mummy* totally has to deal with the whole Arab-Israeli conflict AND with an evil mummy, and by the end he's tight with the native Arabs and Israelians and everything. At least, I think that's who it was. It was set in Egypt but that's just next door to Israel, so it's practically the same place, sort of like how Canada is practically just an American state. So, anyways, Brendan totally makes everyone be all, "Dude, he's scary!" and how does he do that? With his righteously rippling abs? No, it's because he carries some serious bad weaponry. The answer is GUNS. By the end, everyone who is still alive respects him because he is a dead-wicked shot.

Of course, Brendan doesn't just randomly off everyone who makes him totally cheesed. He's like way responsible and tries to save everyone from the tomb when it's going Titanic, even the bad guys. But still, he has the biggest guns of everyone in the movie, and that's why he was able to destroy the mummy and win the girl. So maybe we Americans should

send some cute, buff soldiers to Israel and have them walk around with scary looks on their faces and big guns. Then the Israelians and the Arabs would be all, "Check those scary guns, dude. We've never seen any guns THAT wicked. We'd better stop fighting."

Question: My parents were married in the temple thirty-one years ago, and they just divorced. I can't find any doctrinal assurance that my mother will make it into the celestial kingdom. We know that worthy single women will be given a husband, but what about divorced women?
—Lori Forbes, full-time mom

Answer: That would be so Disney of you to get them back together, like in *The Parent Trap.* You should totally find out what their first date was and then you and your sister could re-create it and just pretend that you needed to talk to each of them and make them meet you somewhere and you could have romantic music.

My friend Kallie isn't allowed to play her *Titanic* CD anymore because her dad is sick of it, so I could borrow it. And you could put black orchids on the table like I heard they had at junior prom and sprinkle the tablecloth with this really cute glitter with hearts in it that I bought in case I ever meet a hot guy and have to send him a card.

If that didn't work you could just be all subtle and drop your mom a really careful hint, like you could say, "Mom, HELLO, check this. You were married for thirty years and that's already an eternity anyway, so you might as well marry Dad again because there's no way you're going to find someone hot to go with because you're already so ancient." Then she'd be all grateful and stuff and probably buy you that sweet Hilfiger skirt you saw at Dillard's last week.

Mahonri the Mormon Psychic

Dear Mahonri: I am an avid genealogist. I spend at least six hours a day on my computer doing family history work, and I have more than two gigabytes of precious data on my drive. A few months ago, I started having problems with corrupted and missing data. Until now I've been able to reconstruct my work, but this past week I've lost so much ground I don't know if I'll ever recover. Can you help?
—Challenged in Chattanooga

Dear Challenged: Sister, take your hands off the keyboard and back away from the computer. Through a special online psychic network to which I have access, I was able to discern that an evil spirit has taken up residence in your central processing unit and is deliberately sabotaging your data so the adversary can keep families apart eternally. My next statement is going to bother a lot of people, but I'm afraid the gateway through which the evil spirit entered your computer was that Harry Potter game you let your grandson play all afternoon last summer when you should have been doing your family history work.

What this computer really needs is the laying on of hands and a stern rebuke.

Say what you want about how uplifting Harry Potter is on some levels, but its fundamental premise is dark, corrupt, and evil. I mean, come on—spells, potions, and magic wands? I've downloaded a healing blessing to your computer, and I'm mailing you a special spiritual defragging crystal that you need to affix atop your CPU with a glue gun. I don't know what kind of relationship you have with your home teachers, but what this computer really needs is the laying on of hands and a stern rebuke.

A Note to My Readers: Since I moved my psychic advice column from *The Panguitch Weekly Advocate* to *The Mormon Tabernacle Enquirer*, I've been most gratified by the response from dozens of new readers.

I'm getting lots of e-mails from you, and I find that your needs and pleas are energizing my spiritual gifts like never before. However, I'm getting too many inappropriate questions along the lines of "When will the Second Coming happen?"

Brothers and sisters, it's beyond my sphere of influence and authority to try to answer questions like those. Please do not exercise your faith in my gifts beyond asking about matters that directly apply to your own individual circumstances. I'm not saying I don't have some impressions about those weightier questions, but it's not my place to share them in this public forum.

On the other hand, neither am I saying that if you go out of your way to talk to me at the next singles home evening, I won't reward you with a hint or two about some rather interesting insights I've gained.

Ask a Beehive

By Mandi Meecham,
age 12
Draper 34th Ward,
Draper Utah
Southeast Stake

Question: We're told we should read the scriptures every day. After a recent sacrament meeting talk when our bishop encouraged us to do so, I set a goal to finally get through the Isaiah parts of the Book of Mormon. But those chapters are really hard! What should I do to keep up and not get lost or bored?

—Margaret Fulsom, realtor

Answer: Dude, I feel your pain. My dad just got called to the high council and the stake president ripped him a new one for not holding family scripture study every day and so he came home sweating and was all, "Kids, we are reading the scriptures every day at six o'clock in the morning and that's final!" Um, hello! Six in the a.m.? I am so completely comatose then, and plus, how harsh can that be when school is over? Could he be any more Hitler? I was all, "Dad, take a Zanax or something. That's sooo not going to happen." So he said he'd buy me a sweet little Cabriolet when I turn sixteen if I am on time to scripture study every day between now and then. I'm stoked about that because there's no way Dad will have the energy to keep this going for longer than like six weeks. He will for sure have gotten over this guilt trip by the time school starts. And until then, I can always go back to bed after scripture study. Plus, adversity is good for the soul. Getting up so early totally makes me understand what the pioneers went through.

So we're reading Second Nephi, and it is way Looney Tunes. Like, what was Isaiah's deal? He seems like this total pill who has

serious issues with women who wear jewelry. Dad read in chapter 13 this morning a weird part that said, "Don't you women even think about wearing tinkling ornaments, and round tires, and chains, and mufflers, and tablets, and mantles, and blah blah blah." And I said, "Dude, what the? Is he talking about women or cars?" and my brother Braxton said, "Or Christmas trees?" and we totally cracked up. Mom opened her can of "You kids need to respect the gospel!" Yeah, okay, Mom, here's the 4-11: if Isaiah could have laid off the wine a little and just written what he meant, in plain English, then maybe Brax and I could pay attention better.

Mahonri the Mormon Psychic

Dear Mahonri: My husband and I are expecting number three! We know we're blessed, but with the expansion of our family we will outgrow the Durango. We can't decide which SUV will best serve our needs. I need a dependable vehicle to bus kids around and something with an all-leather interior for easy cleanup. My husband just wants something to tow the boat. With so many choices, we just can't make up our minds. We've tried praying about it, but we've both received different answers. Is inspiration telling us to get the Yukon or the Expedition? Is one of us more spiritually in tune than the other? We need your guidance!

—Stupefied in Springville

Dear Stupefied: On my way to a psychic fair held at a casino convention center in

Wendover recently, I stopped at some Salt Lake dealerships to test-drive both the Yukon and the Expedition. After pulling over in a parking lot for some prayer and meditation in each vehicle, I found myself leaning toward the Yukon. Though it doesn't have enough interior storage compartments and the glove box is pitifully small, the Yukon handles with the agility of an acrobat and has the stamina of a Clydesdale. The ride felt extremely civilized, not at all truck-like. The Yukon is a winning combination of size, power, maneuverability, and safety.

However, I felt vaguely troubled all during the excellent psychic fair. As I was having my biofeedback interpreted at one booth, it suddenly came to me: At this time, none of the SUVs are right for you. After doing some more psychic work at home, I discovered the reason why: Your husband has been paying tithing only on his net income, not on his gross. Sister, I have discerned that you were not aware of this fact, but nevertheless heaven can't give you the tremendous blessing of a new SUV when your family isn't putting the kingdom first financially. I suggest you have a good heart-to-heart with hubby, and once things are corrected you can hope for a blessing so big there'll scarcely be enough room in your garage to receive it.

Heaven can't give you the tremendous blessing of a new SUV when your family isn't putting the kingdom first financially.

Dear Mahonri: Last Sunday the bishop called me as elders quorum president, and I've spent all week agonizing over who should be in my presidency. I was able to pick my second counselor and secretary without any problem, but the first counselor is giving me fits. I've narrowed it down to two brethren. One is an

outgoing brother who is great at making friends and teaching dynamic lessons, and the other is a quieter guy who always attends every activity. Can you help me decide?
—Torn in Tooele

Dear Torn: I gave this matter considerable ponderation during my weekly visit to the middle of a field where we had an authentic crop circle a few years back. Like you, I was first drawn to the more outgoing brother, who would have provided a good counterbalance to your own exceedingly mellow personality. However, as I reviewed in my mind how the typical elders quorum works and what skills are most needed, I discerned that the quieter brother would be more of an asset to your presidency.

For one thing, he is willing and able to get up early for presidency meetings, while the other brother would blow them off half the time. Even more importantly, the quiet brother will voluntarily spearhead service projects ranging from helping families load their moving trucks to shutting down widows' swamp coolers in the autumn. The outgoing brother? He wouldn't even show up to most service projects, and don't ever bother asking him to help set up or take down chairs. Call him as home-teaching supervisor and let him work the phones on his own time and from the comfort of his own home, since anything more will just disappoint you and incriminate him.

Mormon Horoscope

 ARIES: Endangering your position in the hereafter will be only one of many problems if you don't learn to rein in your ambition and greed. True, Amway has made millions for many, but remember that someone is always buried at the bottom of a pyramid. Learn a new hobby this month. Tatting, glass blowing, or making violas from kits might suit your needs.

 TAURUS: Avoid any food cooked in the church kitchen this month; you know that someone in the Relief Society presidency would love to give you food poisoning. If your home teachers come this month, they'll come unannounced and in the middle of dinner, so keep your curtains down.

 GEMINI: The more yellow you wear, the more others will find you spiritually charismatic, and you may finally get that church calling you've been secretly coveting. Be wary of sharing too much personal information with others, especially on the Internet—gossips lurk everywhere, and you never know what might get said that will land you in the bishop's office.

 CANCER: This is the month to broaden your vocabulary. Everyone loves that firm handshake of yours, but they've grown tired of being "appreciated." Try to "esteem" someone in the ward and "cherish" someone in your family. Life is going to give you a whole bunch of lemons toward the end of the month; make sure you store the sugar now so you can be swimming in lemonade by the time your birthday rolls around.

 LEO: We realize you're obsessed with that mane of yours, Leo, but the right reason to bear your testimony is that your heart is full, not that your hair is full. Make sure those special promptings come from inspiration and not from your mirror. We appreciate that you want to share the love and the sunshine, but try to remember you don't own them in the first place.

 VIRGO: Your attention to detail, one of your greatest assets, is the reason why you are so often made the ward clerk or Relief Society secretary. A little attention to sequence and protocol might benefit you now: make sure you don't send membership records to the Address Unknown File before the person moves or send records marked excommunicated before the court is held.

 LIBRA: A church assignment has been taking too much of your time and energy—find ways to minimize. For starters, you can skip every other early-morning planning meeting. If you're male, the third talk in your next stake priesthood meeting will contain a crucial spiritual message for you, so listen closely. If you're female, every single meeting you attend will contain a crucial spiritual message for you.

 SCORPIO: Someone is going to try and take away your Mountain Dew. Now that you know this, you might be able to prevent it with your incredible charm. If that doesn't work, you may invoke blood atonement to show that no one messes with Scorpio.

 SAGITTARIUS: We realize that frankness is one of your strengths, Sag, but cheerfully telling the bishop his tie was the ugliest thing you've ever seen was not exactly a good idea. Now that spring has arrived, it's time to lay off eating cheddar fishes all through sacrament meeting and channel your natural athleticism into something productive: prepare to be involved big time in church softball all summer long.

 CAPRICORN: You must remember that Stalin, Mao, Elvis, and Joseph Smith were all Capricorns. What sets them apart from each other is the use they made of their leadership talents and how well they heeded inspiration. Your desire to take charge is not entirely evil in and of itself, as long as you beware secret combinations and stay grounded in the scriptures. Do not plot an overthrow of the current elders quorum or Relief Society presidency; remember, many are called but few are chosen.

 AQUARIUS: You will be called on to speak, and you will not be able to get out of it. You're naturally creative and don't mind public speaking, though. So the toughest part will be picking out clothing that will match the caliber of the talk you give. What your ward needs now is an explanation of how astrology helps prove the church is true—and you, Aquarius, are the one to write the talk. Silence all those naysayers who think only heathens read their horoscopes.

 PISCES: It's still unlikely that the Three Nephites will visit you this month—don't you think it's time you quit setting a place for them at the dinner table? You can't hie to Kolob, Pisces, so trying focusing on more mundane concerns. If you don't actually prepare something for the Sunday school lesson you have to teach next week, you're going to get a calling in the nursery and be stuck there for the rest of your life.

Mahonri the Mormon Psychic

Dear Mahonri: I work hard and live the gospel, but I can't seem to get out of poverty. I have my own business watering plants in office buildings, but companies have been cutting back and I can barely afford my own living expenses. I am behind on my rent and child support, and my car is broken. Why don't I receive more blessings?
—Miffed in Monroe

Dear Miffed: Don't forget that attitude of gratitude, my friend. However, I've meditated about your situation, and I agree that your material circumstances are not in proper balance with what you deserve. I have a couple of tips for you.

One, make sure you volunteer to help with your ward's next Deseret Industries drive. Keep your eye out for a red-colored item about the size of a toaster. When you take this item to an antiques appraiser, you'll discover that it is extremely valuable. I have prayed about whether it is okay for you to do this, and I've received a clear vibe that it is acceptable.

Two, I am lending you a special crystal to help you draw upon cosmic forces to improve your material circumstances. This crystal was originally used by a Nephite landowner in about 300 A.D. If you hold it to your forehead each day for several minutes and meditate about material prosperity, you'll be surprised at the good fortune that comes your way. And most importantly, don't forget to keep paying your tithes and offerings!

View from the Valley: Chewing the Gospel Cud
By Rulon S. Wesson

Ever once in a while (more and more it seems), Sister Wesson manages to get me scrubbed and brushed and off to church, even though there's always chores to be done around our place. The bishop, he don't take kindly to excuses from me about missing church, except he didn't mind it much when his old mare foundered and he excused me from a priesthood executive committee meeting to go out to his place and do some horse doctoring. Guess he figured the bishop's horse is like the Lord's horse, so it takes the place of church under them circumstances. I'm okay with that.

Anyway, that ain't what I'm talking about today. It just so happened that last Sunday, I'm sitting there in fast and testimony meeting (which ain't ever fast enough for ol' Rulon, if you catch my drift), when daffy old Sister McMurtrey gets up and starts jawin' away, ruminating on bunions and blessings like there's no tomorrow. I just set there for fifteen minutes with my eyes glazed over, when suddenly I had this vision of my best milk cow, Amelia, standing there at the pulpit, and she's just chewing her old cud, right there in the microphone, same as ol' Sister McMurtrey! It was about then that the Spirit starts trumpeting away in my brain, and I know I've stumbled over a principle of the gospel.

See, a cow's belly ain't built to digest the hay the first time it goes down. It ain't ready yet. The cow, she chews it up, swallows it, and lets it set there deep down in her gullet for a few hours. Then later, she lies around and horks it all back up in the form of a soggy wad, and she chews on it some more until it's ready to swallow again. After doing that for a time or two, the cow turns the hay into more beef or else leaves it lying around the pasture for ol' Rulon to step around.

Keep chewing the gospel cud, and you'll end up swallowing it all, by and by.

It's the same way with the gospel. First time you read the scriptures or learn your Sunday school lessons, you pretty much just got to swallow them whole, 'cause they don't make a hell of a lot a sense half the time. That's the thing, see—it takes time for the spirit to digest it. So that's what church does. It helps us cough up what we learned, chew on it again and again, and swallow it back down. Your bishop, he's a clever guy, and he knows what it takes to help us finally get the message of the gospel through our thick skulls, so he makes sure we talk about the same things every week or so. Same as with the rest of the church, like general conference and the *Ensign*. Every time we chew that cud, we get closer and closer to making it a part of us, same as cows.

Before I understood that principle, sometimes I would just roll over when Sister Wesson tried haulin' my carcass out a bed on Sunday morning, and I'd say to her, "The church is true, so's the Book a Mormon, and Joseph Smith was a prophet, pay your tithing and say your prayers and do your home teaching. There. I just done church. Now go back to sleep." Never worked, but it was worth a try. But now I understand the cud principle, and so I have to think of different excuses. And it still don't work.

Sometimes people are stupid like cows, and they'll swallow all kinds of dangerous things, like thinking gay folks ought to be able to get hitched or that we got no business bombing the Arabs back to the Stone Age. Rulon's advice is to make sure you're always getting the right feed. Stick to reading the scriptures and churchy books. If you need news, read the *Church News* or at least the *Deseret News* and leave it at that. If you get a hankerin' for a movie, there's lots a good church movies out these days, or conference reruns. That's good feed, brothers and sisters. Anything else, and you'll bloat. Keep chewing the gospel cud, and you'll end up swallowing it all, by and by.

Ask a Beehive

By Mandi Meecham,
age 12
Draper 34th Ward,
Draper Utah
Southeast Stake

Question: I just heard from my husband, who likes to study church history, that the Word of Wisdom requirements weren't mandatory for the temple recommend until the early twentieth century. Is this true?
—Verne Katz, realtor

Answer: Okay, like, if you're going to get all freaked about the olden Mormons drinking beer and chewing tobacco, then hello—you obviously don't know much about the olden-days prophets. They were totally mental. And they did waaay worse things than horking down a few lagers.

So, like check this. Me and my Young Women group went to Salt Lake the other night for an activity to see the Lion and Beehive Houses. At first I was all, "Oh, thank you. Something historical and educational. Could you please bore me some more?" I

mean, HELLO? Young Women activities are supposed to be ALL fun ALL the time. But then Lindsay was all, "Check it, girlfriend— we'll be right near the Gateway." Sweet. The Earring Hut has these killer amber goldfish earrings that so have my name on them. And it is soooo not hard to ditch my Young Women leaders. Sister Carlyle has asthma, and Sister Norbert is way huge and totally ancient—like thirty-seven or something.

Anyways, Lindsay and I were all, "Dude, we can totally blow through the houses and then cruise to Gateway," so we went. And the houses are like totally whacked! It way blew my mind. I mean, if you're all freaking out over those ancient Mormons sucking down beers, then this will totally freak you out: Some of the prophets had MORE THAN ONE WIFE. Like, twelve wives all at the same time! That is totally sick!

You obviously don't know much about the olden-days prophets. They were totally mental.

And it gets weirder—there's this little cafeteria-type thing in the basement of the house too! So like what's with THAT? Did the kids have to pay for meals? Did the wives have a little side business going, selling bread and Snickers and stuff to pay for all the kids? I'm not a poindexter or anything, but it seems like prophets should have only ONE wife. And they shouldn't try to make money on the side by starting up a cafeteria and making their kids pay for their food.

Anyway, so that's why I don't study church history too hard. It's okay to study SOME things really hard, like the scriptures or something, I guess—whatever—but you don't want to look at other things too close.

Editorial: There's a Lot We Could Learn from the Moonies

By Euella Partridge

About a year ago, my husband LeVoy was asked by President Bush to serve as assistant undersecretary for environmental and labor coordination, and so we moved from Orem to Washington, D.C. I don't know what you think, but we've met some wonderful Christian people out here: the Roves, the DeLays, the Gingriches, and the Santorums, and that lovely Ann Coulter. Good Christian folk, every one. And I've gotten to be pretty good friends with some people who belong to the Unification Church of Pastor Sun Myung Moon.

We know that there exists some truth in all religions and that we can and should try to learn from people of all faiths. Well, I've been thinking about Pastor Moon and his church recently, and I think we Mormons could learn a lot from them.

I know that in some circles Pastor Sun Myung Moon may not necessarily seem like someone we could learn much from. After all, he's Korean. But what a lot of people don't know is that there are a lot of similarities between our Mormon beliefs and his Unification beliefs and that he's done a lot of good in the world. For one thing, since we've been living here in Washington, I've discovered that the Unification Church people are pretty much all Republicans, like us. They've even got their own newspaper, the *Washington Times*, just like we have the *Deseret News* in Utah. And nobody was more eager to attack that immoral traitor Bill Clinton than the *Washington Times*. Or more eager to praise President Bush, either. And

you'd be amazed at how many Unificationers are in the Bush administration! Way more than us Mormons, I can tell you that!

But it's not just politically that we have a lot in common. Do you know that Pastor Moon is against homosexuals? He's totally against them. He says that if he gets elected president of Korea or whatever, he'll have them all put to death. He says that Jews will have to be converted to Christ at the time of the Second Coming, and he says the Holocaust was God punishing them for killing Jesus. Well, I'm not so read up on my Book of Mormon and all, but that sounds kinda like us.

They have some rules that just make all sorts of sense, the more you think about them.

When it comes to sexual things, we're even more alike than you'd think. For example, Pastor Moon is totally against sex outside of marriage, just like we are. But they have some other beliefs this one guy was telling me about. Like, Pastor Moon wants married couples to have a picture of him over the bed, so that when they make love they're thinking of him, and so he's sort of symbolically watching everything they do. I think that's a real special idea, and I'm planning to talk to LeVoy and see how he'd feel if we did the same with a picture of President Hinckley.

They have some other rules that just make all sorts of sense, the more you think about them. This is a little embarrassing, but I'm trying to make a point here. Like, for example, the first two times a married couple has relations, Pastor Moon says that the woman should be on top. That's sort of symbolic of the Garden of Eden and the apple and the snake and all, where she knew more than he did. But then ever after that, the man should be on top, because he presides now that we're not in Eden anymore. What we call the "missionary position" he calls the "dominion position," which, when you think about it, is a lot more appropriate name for it.

Now, they believe in these group marriage things, where you don't know the person you're marrying beforehand and three hundred couples all get married at once. And I don't hold with those kinds of practices, of course. But the way it was explained to me, even that made sense. Shouldn't your spouse be chosen for you by God? And shouldn't you let someone you think of as a prophet speak for God on our behalf? Personally, I try to imagine if President Hinckley had gotten a revelation for our daughter Kimmie about who she should marry. I'm sure it would have been better for her than marrying that Ronald Spichelin guy, who she absolutely refuses to dump no matter how much we try to convince her.

So all in all, I think we have a whole lot in common with the Unification Church, and we should think of Pastor Moon as someone pretty darn close to the truth. Because, you know, being here in Washington and all, I've gotten real interested in politics, and I read a lot of what Pastor Moon says politically, and you know what? You can't tell his writings from Ezra Taft Benson's at all.

Ask a Beehive
By Mandi Meecham, age 12
Draper 34th Ward, Draper Utah
Southeast Stake

Question: The other day in high priest quorum, a guy I was sitting next to said we don't have to worry about pollution or recycling because the earth will be restored to its Edenic glory. It sounds kind of fishy to me, but other people were pretty convinced. What do you think?
—Russell Ewert, asset manager

Answer: Okay, like I had to do this one project for social studies where I had to choose an environmental topic and research it and stuff and solve the problem, and at first I was all "This is sooo Nyquil. I'm sure. Could I be more bored?" but then Mrs. Lansing gave me Jared Hunter as a partner and then I was TRIPPING because he's in eighth grade and a varsity cheerleader for our junior high team and once in this pep rally he pulled off his shirt and his abs are sooo ripped! They are BAD! So I was all "whoo-hoo!" even though Jared's face isn't all that cute. It's all about his abs. And his spirit and personality, of course.

So anyway we were just chilling one night at his house and he turned on some show on PBS—it was called *Novo* or something—and it showed all these cute whales and how everyone is trying to off them, and I totally got into it. I was all, "Jared, they're so cute! We should save the whales!" and he said something about how we should save them because they're good eating, and I thought that was totally sick! But then he said he was just psyching me out and he kissed me—SERIOUSLY, don't tell my dad—and we decided to do our project on whales and we totally bagged an A.

In Sunday school we learned that man has unrighteous dominion over the animals and stuff, and so I totally think that we need to walk it if we talk it. We need to not hurt animals and not wear fur and not wear leather—unless you find REALLY cute leather shoes or a jacket and you just have to buy it, especially if it's on sale—and not wear makeup that's been tested on animals, except that sometimes you can't tell, so my advice is just don't read your makeup labels! Then you don't have to feel guilty about it.

Ask a Beehive

By Mandi Meecham,
age 12
Draper 34th Ward,
Draper Utah
Southeast Stake

Question: My bishop says they don't mention R-rated movies in the new For the Strength of Youth *pamphlet because they're trying to teach us correct principles rather than the letter of the law. Is it OK to watch some R-rated movies now?*

—*Ben Murdock, priest quorum secretary*

Answer: I can sooo answer this one. Freaking out about R-rated movies is like seriously my parents' main hobby in life, and I have seen them go postal on it so many times that I am a total expert on the subject. This is so freaky because just this week for family home evening the parentals launched into their whole "Don't watch R-rated movies!" song and dance once again. So this question is like cosmic karma or something.

So anyway, Dad had baked this pan of brownies for family home evening and he was all, "Do these look good? Do you want some? I used only the finest ingredients in these brownies," and Braxton, who is ten and TOTALLY naïve, said, "Yeah! Score me some brownies, dude!" So Dad ignored the fact that Brax called him "dude"—he hates that—and got this big smirk on his face. He was all, "OK, but there's just one thing I have to tell you: I used just a TINY bit of dog poop in here. Just a tiny bit. The rest of the brownies are really good." And so of course Brax, the feeb, said just what Dad wanted him to: "Dude, gross! That's totally sick!" And then Dad goes into the big "This is just like R-rated movies! They are mostly good but have a few bad parts! Blah blah blah!"

OK, so maybe this is impressive if you're ten, like Brax, but I'm twelve and I've seen this kind of analogy twice in Young Women, four times in Primary, and once in Sunday school. I have seriously seen seven pans of poo brownies. So, my bad, but I was totally not cool with Dad's little show and tell. Anyway, while they were going on about how R-rated movies are evil, I totally fought down the temptation to say, "But what's the big deal about seeing a pile of dog poo in a movie? Why is that so terrible?" It totally killed off my Sunday school class when I said that, and Danny Menser laughed so hard he cried, but Brother Vale was all ticked off. And if I tick off the parentals during FHE, they go into lecture mode and we're all stuck there for the next two hours. And *Grey's Anatomy* is on after FHE, so that's not a go. But, really, you'd think they would know that cable TV is completely R-rated and it's never killed any of us yet. Besides, if you really want to score some smut, you just hit the PG-13 movies. That's where it's at these days.

I have seriously seen seven pans of poo brownies.

So Brax was all, "I'm never, ever going to see an R-rated movie ever, Mom and Dad! Thanks!" He may have meant it, but he also knows that acting sincere is the best way to score the biggest piece of dessert, and he knew that Mom had made a pan of non-poo brownies. I decided to just make them happy and said, "That was a way impressive analogy! I've never seen poo brownies before!" I think that's one of those little white lies that heaven will totally understand.

Guest Column: I Resent Being Stereotyped
By Nickie Johnston

I am sooo tired of being labeled a "typical Utah Mormon mother" by just about everyone I see! Even if they don't call me that, I can see that people look at me, smirk, judge me unrighteously, and then move on. I'm sure they think I'm a total Mormon stereotype, and I think this kind of prejudging is totally unfair!

For example, just yesterday I was driving my four kids—Connor, Tanner, Kylee, and Kayla—to their soccer practices, and I saw someone smiling at my minivan. Okay, so I drive a minivan, but it's not a Mormon minivan! Every other mother in my neighborhood drives a Dodge Caravan, and mine is a Dodge Caravan XLS. It's a totally different model and has extra features and everything. Plus, everyone else's Caravan is green, and mine is forest green. Totally different color palette.

And then there's the matter of hobbies. Take scrapbooking, for instance. Every Mormon mother scrapbooks, it seems, but not me. I create memory books instead. It's a totally different hobby, and the end results have a completely different feel. I tried to explain that to the woman at the craft store, but she just smirked and said, "Whatever. Look, do you want your scrapbooker discount card or not?" I had a hard time not getting huffy, I can tell you that!

Seriously, memory books are totally different. I'll show you mine sometime so you can see.

Also, it seems like every Mormon mother I know who's my age has the exact same hair: brown, streaked with blond, chin-length, layered, and flipped out just a little. Well, my hair is not streaked. It's highlighted. And it's not flipped out, either. It's called "bent." Bending your hair is a totally different look from the flip-do. Totally different! And I have these teeny little wispy bangs. But just last week my visiting teacher Kari told me that I look exactly like Connie Manning, who lives down the street from me, and she wanted to know if we were sisters! I was totally shocked! Connie streaks, she doesn't highlight, and it turns out that we are related, but she's only my second cousin. We could not be more different people if we tried!

I'll have to start making some really radical changes, like buying my LDS romance novels at Seagull Book instead of Deseret Book.

And then there are my kids. Conner and Tanner do play soccer like all their friends, it's true, but they're goalies rather than guards or lineman or whatever those guys who run a lot are called. Goalies are so different, it's like they play a different sport—not really soccer at all. And Kylee and Kayla do not take ballet like all their friends. They take a class called Ballet with a Modern Twist.

No matter how different I am, though, people still judge me. Just last week the bishop suggested in Relief Society that we read a recent *Ensign* talk because it was "directed at lightening the burdens of typical Mormon mothers," and he looked right at me! How on earth can he think I'm typical?

I'm tired of being lumped in with all the other women in my neighborhood. I guess I'll have to start making some really radical changes, like buying my LDS romance novels at Seagull Book instead of Deseret Book. And maybe I'll start saying "ah-men" instead of "amen."

That should do it.

View from the Valley: Bag That Trophy Testimony

By Rulon S. Wesson

This time of year, my thoughts turn to the wonder of the great outdoors and I ponder the glories of God's creation, what with watching the leaves turn from green to gold, hearing the sound of a hard frost crunching beneath my boots, and tracking a blood trail from that trophy bull elk that's got my arrow stuck in his shoulder.

You know, growing up in the mountains of Idaho, I was taught that every good thing in life points to the Savior. The other weekend, as I worked my way along the ridge following the sound of that thrashing elk, I got to thinking, "This blood I'm following, it reminds me that were it not for the blood of the Savior, there wouldn't be no gospel at all." That's when it occurred to me that gaining a testimony is exactly the same as hunting a big ol' bull. Next thing I know, I'm feeling about the same as Enos, having a downright spiritual moment while hunting the beasts of the forest.

So looky here. If you want a trophy elk, you got to prepare. You make sure your rifle's oiled, get some camo coveralls and a four-wheeler, and you might even sprinkle elk urine on yourself so they can't smell you coming. With a testimony, it's kind of the same, but without the urine. You got to make sure you have the right equipment, like your Book of Mormon and the rest of the scriptures. You'll want a sharp red marking pencil (which, coincidently, is shaped a lot like an arrow, and the red tip—well, that's what an arrow looks like when you pull it out of the

critter you just killed. I'm telling you, the parallels would be scary if it wasn't so dang spiritual). You'll be needing a white shirt and tie, and you oughta knock the manure off your boots before you go to church. Church is where testimonies bed down, so yup, you're gonna have to go.

When you get up to your favorite hunting spot, you probably say a little prayer, right? Mine usually goes something like, "Father'n Heaven, you know the intentions of my heart, and though I sometimes cuss and I ain't always been the best home teacher in the world, I'd still love to get me that elk I seen up here last Sund—er, last weekend, so if you wouldn't mind leading me to it, I'd be much obliged." But see, if you want a big ol' testimony, you got to do the same as Joseph Smith and pray that you'll find one like his. And just where did Joseph go to get his testimony in the first place? Weren't no fancy-shmancy church with no stained-glass windows, was it? Nope, he went to the woods, out with the critters. Don't it just send chills down your spine?

Gaining a testimony is exactly the same as hunting a big ol' bull elk.

Next, you need a guide who knows where that big bull hides and knows how to put you in range. For your testimony, the guide is the Holy Ghost, of course. You already got your guide when you got baptized, so why not put the bugger to use? Your guide will know right where to find your trophy testimony, and as he eases you over that last hump, he'll whisper in that still, small voice, "There it is, son"—or "missy," since I don't guess we want to leave out the womenfolk!—"he's yours for the taking." When you finally bag it, your heart will just swell up in your bosom to overflowing and you'd probably weep were it not for the fact that your buddies would make you feel kinda girly! Too bad you can't get your picture took with your trophy testimony like you can with your elk.

Now then, you want your testimony to last forever, like your trophy bull, so you got to take care of some business. For an elk, you got to make sure you protect the head without tearing up the cape around the neck. That's why you made a lung shot and not a head shot. With your testimony, you want to make sure you stay far away from stuff that's gonna ruin your head, like reading anti-Mormon books or going to R-rated movies. You might hear people talk about polygamy and stuff, and you just plug your ears. Trust old Rulon on this one.

Once you pack him out, you got to take your bull to a reputable taxidermist so you're sure to have him around for years of enjoyment. With your testimony, unfortunately you can't just stuff it and hang it on the wall; you got to always take care of it, enduring to the end as they say. But don't be ashamed to trot it out regular like and show it to other people. I think the scriptures say something like, "Don't go keeping your head-mount under a box or nuthin'. Keep it out where the world can see it." Folks'll appreciate you sharing it with them. Hell, maybe they'll go get one of their own! How great'll be your joy then?

Kraft Korner: Scrapbooking Your Excommunication
By Kelly C. Sherwin

Fellow scrapbookers unite! Ladies, this column is just for you! So put down that dishrag (we all know you were just pretending to wash dishes anyway!) and get out that boxful of precious photos. Let's talk about scrapbooks. They're way more fun than driving kids to soccer practice, and when Hubby gets grumpy because dinner's not on the table, you can say, "Honey, I'm working on our family history!" What a perfect excuse for indulging in a super-fun hobby!

We've all seen tons of cute baptism scrapbook pages, cute baby blessing pages, and cute temple wedding pages. And I've seen so many darling missionary scrapbooks lately that it makes me almost want to go on a mission just for the scrapbook possibilities (or the "scrap-abilities!"). But I digress. I want to talk to you about how to scrapbook one of those little oopsies that life hands out from time to time—excommunication!

Now, before you say, "That Sherilyn sure is up in the night," let me remind you that we Mormons have been commanded to preserve all our memories for our progeny, not just the happy ones. Excommunication can be a great learning experience for all people involved, and preserving it in a scrapbook gives us a chance to "accentuate the positive" (don't you just love *The Jungle Book*?).

Here are a few tips to help make your excommunication page the envy of the neighborhood:

1. Capture the event. Try to be present at the disciplinary council when the verdict is announced. If you can slip into the room ▶

unnoticed, so much the better! Use a camera with a good zoom lens so you can get a close-up of the newly exed person's face when the verdict is read. Get a picture of the stake president as he reads the verdict. If possible, get individual pictures of everyone involved in the disciplinary council. If you know you won't be able to sneak in for a picture or two, give your camera to a council member ahead of time (make him some cookies as a thank-you afterward!). Remember: photos that capture the emotion of the moment will make for a more memorable page.

> **Excommunication can be a great learning experience for all people involved, and preserving it in a scrapbook gives us a chance to "accentuate the positive."**

2. **Use a catchy title.** Now's a great time to be creative! Examples of good titles for your excommunication page are "Look Who's Been Outed!" "Porn Doesn't Pay!" "Troop Leader No Longer!" and "If Only My Zipper Had Gotten Stuck." Look through your scriptures or use your Topical Guide to find commandments that relate to the excommunication, and handwrite or print them in a cute font to enhance the page.

3. **Embellish with funky accents.** While you can usually find a wide range of stickers, die-cuts, or paper for just about any theme you can imagine, it's really hard to find excommunication-related page embellishments. The "Damn, I'm Bad" line is coming out with a cute "The Seven Cardinal Sins" group of stickers later this fall (look for them at Scrap 'N Grin). But in the meantime, go through your own supplies and see what you have. For instance, you can cut out some cute horns and put them on top of a Paperkins doll to make a devil. Or you can make flam-

ing words: use deckle-edged scissors and red-and-black paper for piecing together your page's title. You can also download flaming fonts for free—try myevilfonts.com.

4. **Get other points of view.** Because an excommunication is such an emotional time, everyone involved is sure to have a strong opinion on the subject. Be sure to have everyone on the disciplinary council write a message to the newly exed person. I saw a cute page last week that everyone on the council had signed. It was full of messages like "Hearing what you did made me physically ill," "I never believed Satan truly walked among us until tonight," and "I used to think it was impossible to do something so bad that God would stop loving you." Memorable for sure!

An excommunication page can really add that special something to your LDS scrapbook. Just imagine how proud your exed spouse, child, or parent will be to see his or her accomplishments immortalized in your scrapbook for all to see! What a great (and fun!) way to preserve those unforgettable memories for generations to come. Until next time, happy scrappin'!

Sherilyn is a long-time scrapbooking instructor at her Orem, Utah, store Scrap 'N Grin. She has authored an LDS-themed scrapbooking idea book called Oh, Heavens! How Scrapbooking Can Get You Closer to God. *Her syndicated column, Kraft Korner, runs in four different newspapers along Utah's Wasatch Front.*

Opposition in All Things
Today's Debate: Are Riches a Blessing or a Curse?

Riches Are Blessings from Heaven
By Gerald P. Cunningham, investment banker

You'll hear a lot of contrary opinions, especially in Sunday school, but I remain strong in my convictions: riches are a sign that heaven loves you. I say that if you want to check your righteousness, just check your bank account.

Oh, I know, there's a lot of hooey in the Book of Mormon about being "poor in spirit" and how that state is somehow "blessed." Someone always brings up that scripture whenever the Sunday school chat gets going on riches. And someone else always tells us, with a sternly shaken finger, that riches always lead to pride, which always leads to a downfall. And that's usually when I lose interest and begin daydreaming about the next luxury cruise my wife and I will take. Because, really, pride is not a problem I have to worry about, ever. I prefer to think of myself as justifiably pleased with my own efforts rather than "proud," whatever that means.

After all, I'm the one who earned my money. When other people thank heaven for their material blessings, I have to laugh. Did an angel come down and tell me to invest in Apple computers? Did he earn that Dartmouth MBA? Did he slave in perpetual sleep deprivation to climb the corporate ladder at HFI Finance in my place? I did the hard work to earn the stuff, but I was blessed with the fortitude to do that work, because heaven likes me better than those lazy poor people.

Poor people will tell you that their state is somehow "nobler" than mine. They claim that their blessings come in non-monetary ways. Who do they think they're fooling? So all those middle-class types would rather drive around in their Geo Prizms full of Kool-aid packets and generic shampoo from the dollar store, would they? Well, they can keep their non-monetary blessings, whatever they are. I prefer my blessings the way they are: tangible and with easy ATM access.

Poverty Is a Blessing from Heaven
By Maria S. Martinez, grocery bagger

They'll never admit it, but deep, deep down, rich people are miserable. All of them. They may gleefully drive around town in their super-fancy Cadillac cars and wear their fur coats while you bag groceries. They may even laugh at you in the checkout line, but it's just their way of crying out for attention and love.

I'm glad to be poor because Jesus was poor. He was able to do so much good for others only because He didn't have material possessions to burden him. That's just like me. I can't drive the young women in my ward to camp because I don't have a car, but I can bless their lives in a much better way. For instance, I provide them a much better example of righteousness than their snobby Young Women president who lives in the rich part of the ward. Talking to her makes me glad I am poor, because she always smiles at me in a completely fake way. That's what being rich does to you.

Every night I pray, "Thank you for making me poor! Thank you for making me better than my rich brothers and sisters!" Taking ▶

the bus to work and not owning a TV have made me much more righteous than the rich people in our ward, who are all full of pride.

So they can keep their granite countertops, their big-screen TVs, their DVD players, their fancy Dodge Durangos, and their ski outfits. I was made poor because I'm better than all of them, and I want to stay that way.

Ask a Beehive

By Mandi Meecham, age 12
Draper 34th Ward, Draper Utah Southeast Stake

Question: If it's not a Sunday but you're fasting anyway, is it appropriate to bob for apples? I'm fasting for my grandma this Thursday, but I've also been invited to a party that day, and we're going to bob for apples. Mom thinks I shouldn't go, but I pointed out that I don't have to eat the apples. And we're commanded to adopt a cheerful countenance (as opposed to a "sad countenance") while fasting (Matt. 6: 16–18).
—Devin Naylor, tenth-grade student

Answer: Bobbing for apples is a totally good diet tip because apples are way good for you and if you really get into the whole bobbing thing, it's like aerobics. So you can burn calories and lose weight while having fun at the same time. Seriously, it's like way more fun than kickboxing, which is SO way overrated and stupid. Stacee and I had this free pass for seven kickboxing classes at her country club, because her brother Garritt used to work there and got them to keep her quiet when she was going to tell her mom about the Victoria's Secret catalogs she found in Garritt's closet. So anyways we went to these kickboxing classes and they were way lame. The woman teacher was all muscled, which is gross because boys won't date you if they think you can beat them up. Muscles on a woman are so wrong. And she was all mean, too. Like the first part of the class was just like that aerobics class I took last summer when I was all obsessed about being a cheerleader, but then she was all, "Okay, punch toward the mirror! Punch! Pretend someone is there that you don't like!" and all I could think of was Brayden, this guy in my social science class who's a total player and who dissed Lindsee BAD last year. It was so cruel. But then I was all, "But Brayden's pretty hot," and suddenly I didn't feel like pretending to punch him anymore, and then it struck me how violent this stupid class was, and I was just all sad that we as a society have gotten so we have to punch pretend people in kickboxing all the time. I mean how sad is THAT! It's totally a sign of these latter days that the prophets all talk about.

It's totally a sign of these latter days that the prophets all talk about.

I think apples have like gluecrose or stuckrose or some other kind of science-y word for sugar in them, so I don't know if apples are good diet food or not.

Guest Column: Remember, Honey, You're Always Number Two with Me

By Martin J. Wood

Before I leave to perform my duties as stake president, I just want to reassure you, honey: you'll always be number two with me.

Yep, don't you worry. Ever since that day so long ago on the temple lawn, when I proposed to you, I've made it very clear that you would always come in a solid second. "Honey," I said, with tears in my eyes, "the church will always be first in my life, but I want you to take the second spot."

I was so overcome when you accepted me. It was a great day in my life. And two minutes later, when I drove off to do my home teaching, I was still thinking about my commitment to the church and how you'd be right next in line. And will we ever forget our honeymoon at the welfare farm? What a wonderful way to start a marriage.

I'm sure you remember my diligence in earning my law degree. After all, I had to fulfill my priesthood duty to earn money and respect for our family and the church. I'd come home so tired from my studies, but there you'd be, sometimes still in your Denny's uniform, cooking up dinner for our four children and me. We didn't have a lot, but we made the money stretch. And somehow we scraped enough together to get me that Italian lambs-wool suit with gold cufflinks so I could fulfill my calling as Sunday school president in appropriate clothing. We had just enough left over to buy you the nicest dress on the five-dollar rack at DI.

I don't think you could deny that through all our years together, I've always kept my word. I never forgot to put you right up there in second place. Remember all those years when I was a bishop, and the years before that I spent as elders quorum president? I always got to you second. For instance, remember our eighth anniversary? Remember my diligence when I forsook our dinner date and left you with our lovely children to attend the stake public relations meeting? But on the way home I picked some flowers from the church flowerbed for you and kicked in an extra ten bucks the next time I paid tithing.

"Will we ever forget our honeymoon at the welfare farm? What a wonderful way to start a marriage."

I enjoy recounting that incident in stake conference to inspire the other priesthood holders to be so dedicated. Someday I hope to share it in a session of general conference, though I'm sure by then I'll have better examples to illustrate gospel principles, perhaps even examples that would warrant an onscreen visual aid.

Maybe I could share that time when we gave the money you had saved for your little college courses to the Friends of Scouting, making us Golden Eagle contributors. Or my tears when you called me from the hospital to tell me about the birth of our twins. I was so excited, I told everyone at the elders quorum reactivation bowling activity about it.

No, don't speak, honey. I can see it all in the tears streaming down your face. This always happens when I recount my diligence. You're so grateful to have a man who sticks by his promise, who always exalts his wife to her proper place. Second. Right after the church.

And I promise, honey, I promise to always do so. You're worth it. Roast beef for dinner tonight, okay?

Poet's Corner

Ode to Me, Ward Clerk
by Eric Palmatier

I am the ward clerk.
I am everyone's go-to guy.
You come to me when you need something
  simple, like paperclips.
You come to me every time I finally get
  a chance to spend a Sunday with the
  wife.
You call at weird times, looking for the
  bishop—
Do you think he lives with me or something?
Oh, you're looking for his keys!
I'm tired of your whining that I don't print
  new Relief Society rosters every time
  someone moves in or out.
I'm tired of your bugging me for a print-
  out of every sister's birthday while
  I'm counting heads during sacrament
  meeting.
Can't you see I'm busy?

I have to sit through boring bishopric
  meetings.
I get to sit up front when both counselors
  and the executive secretary are out of
  town.
I have top-level access on the computer.
  Ha!
Do you have the power to make old Sister
  Zupert die in the church's records?
I can have the financial secretary take
  away your budget.
I can inundate your in-box with extra
  paperwork.
I can sabotage your home teaching reports.
You should call me President!

Ask Polygamous Polly

Dear Polly: I'm in a real bind. I've been dating two girls here at BYU, and I'm attracted to them both. They are each beautiful and dedicated to the gospel. One's an elementary ed major, and the other is in family sciences. Both can cook and keep house. I gotta come clean, Polly, I don't know which to choose. Can you help?
—Befuddled at BYU

Dear Befuddled: After thinking over your predicament, I have come up with a possibility that may surprise you, but I think in the end it will work out. Have you ever considered polygamy as your answer? It's a wonderful system that allows for men to bring multiple righteous women into heaven and for those women to learn to share their husband and love each other. It's worked for a lot people. Why don't you give it a try? I can hook you up with some people who could give you few pointers.

Dear Polly: I never knew I could get into a situation as bad as this. I just found out that my eighteen-year-old daughter is pregnant with the child of my live-in boyfriend. How can it be that they've been having an affair behind my back? I'm seriously considering kicking my daughter out of the house because I love my boyfriend and don't want our relationship to end. Any advice?
—Gentile in Georgia

Dear Gentile: Don't kick out the poor girl. It's all perfectly natural. Why, I've known girls to get pregnant at thirteen. And they were so happy, as was the father. Take the plunge into polygamy. You and your daughter will find your relationship growing stronger as you become sister wives. Just make sure you're the first wife.

You and your daughter will find your relationship growing stronger as you become sister wives.

Dear Polly: What do I do? I'm surrounded by beautiful women! They're all in various states of undress, and each is beckoning me to her room. I can't take all of them . . . can I?

—Lost in Las Vegas

Dear Lost: Of course you can, dear. And may God bless you with many offspring.

Dear Polly: Giant insects from Jupiter are attacking the earth. We've destroyed a few with nuclear weapons and lasers, but there are too many of them. In just a few hours the entire planet will be overrun by the monsters, snapping people in half with their vise-like jaws, impaling innocents on their thorny feet, injecting their victims with vile poisons before sucking out their blood and leaving their withered corpses to rot in the vermin-infested streets. For the love of heaven, Polly, what should we do?

—Panicked in the Pentagon

Dear Panicked: Polygamy.

Staff Biographies

David Patton Benson: David came to the *Enquirer* following a long and distinguished career as a pharmacist/actuary and CIA operative. He has served the church in a variety of callings, including financial clerk, materials center supervisor, and stake financial clerk. Wives include Bonnie Holladay Benson, Betsy Milhous Benson, and Bonita Alvarez Benson, all deceased, and his current spouse, Brooke McCarthy Benson. He has fifteen children, stepchildren, and foster children.

Terrill W. Cannon: Born in Vernal, Utah, and raised in Rigby, Idaho, Terrill served in the Army press corps in Vietnam before returning to ranch work in southeastern Idaho. He nearly finished a degree in agronomy at Utah State before taking a job with the Utah Department of Transportation. He is currently retired and splits his time between the *Enquirer* and his duties as a campground host for the Utah Division of State Parks.

Kylee-Ashlee Cannon Christiansen: Kylee-Ashlee was born in Provo, Utah, where she led a life as sheltered from evil as her home valley is sheltered by mountains. After graduating from Provo High School as seminary president, she attended BYU–Idaho for three-and-a-half years, almost attaining a home and family science degree before marrying her eternal companion, a worthy RM named Ammon Wilford Christiansen. "An M.R.S. is more important than a B.S.!" she likes to tell the Beehives in her Layton 34th Ward. Sister Christiansen loves to read her scriptures, get manicures, and sing Primary songs. She is the proud mother of three precious children.

Jack B. Kimball: Born and raised in Scipio, Utah, Jack served as editor of his ward newsletter for seven years before accepting a calling as compiler and editor of the stake annual history, which directly led to his position as an *Enquirer* reporter. He holds a certificate in taxidermy from Stevens-Henager College, collects nineteenth-century buttons, and cultivates the silk for making his own Sunday neckties. A descendent of Martin Harris who has never misplaced any paperwork, he started a statewide union for ward financial clerks to demand better working conditions, particularly at tithing settlement time. He lives with his wife and eight children in Bluffdale, Utah.

Lisa Layton: Lisa's first calling was serving as her MIA Maid class president. Later she was a family home evening group leader in her institute ward at the University of Arizona. In 1991–92 she served a mission in Belgium. Upon returning, she was called as a Relief Society teacher, a position she held until she made the mistake of mentioning in one of her lessons that Joseph Smith practiced polygamy. A special spirit, she enjoys knitting, sewing, baking, canning, and gardening, but she is happy to leave genealogy research to someone else, unless scrapbooking counts as genealogy.

LeVoy Mann: Born in Ogden, Utah, LeVoy grew up in Pocatello, Idaho, where he earned a little money as a ticket taker at the local theater. His love of Hollywood steered him to a degree in performing arts. He became a reporter and entertainment critic after severely injuring his groin in an *American Idol*-related stampede. A dedicated opponent of illegal immigration, he began the Utah chapter of the Minutemen. On weekends, he can usually be found setting traps and target-practicing on the southern borders of Utah. In his spare time he enjoys bee wrangling and theater. LeVoy is president of his elders quorum and lives with his mother in Centerville, Utah.

M. Spencer Pratt: Spencer teaches Gospel Doctrine in the Dadodo Branch on Guam. Born in Burley, Idaho, he is the great-great-great-grandson of James Henstrom, an 1832 convert who once spit-shined Joseph Smith's boots. Spencer holds a B.A. from Idaho State University and taught junior high for fifteen years. A resident of Guam since 1989, he is currently self-employed in the snake-control industry. He served in the Taiwan mission from 1974–76 and is still looking for his eternal companion.

Milton P. Romney: Born on a farm near Cedar City, Utah, Milton was home-schooled by his faithful mothers, alongside the other 27 children living in the family compound. A student at Dixie College since 1987, Milt has studied ancient Hebraic culture and art, Near Eastern architecture, and Babylonian literary structure, none of which are offered at Dixie. Milt was a frequent contributor to the college paper's letters to the editor section before joining the *Enquirer* staff, and he lives with his wives and children in an undisclosed location somewhere in Southern Utah or Arizona.

Teancum Zenos Smoot IV: Brother Smoot wishes to thank all those who have supported him in the writing of his *Enquirer* articles, including Mary, Bathsheba, Juanita, and the children they bore in the rearing up of his mighty kingdom: Adam, Able, Hagar, Moses, Rachel, Joshua, Daniel, Hepsuba, Punctuality, Aha, Behold He Comes With a Sword, the quintuplets, the runty one, and the others, whom he really looks forward to meeting when he is released.

Molly Thatcher Woodruff: Molly has a B.S. degree in child development and family relations with a minor in appropriateness and a certificate from the Miss Manners school. She grew up in Anaheim with lots of exposure to good Disney values and appropriate Disney show tunes. She has been married for more than twenty years to her husband Manfred, "Manny" for short, named after his pioneer ancestors. They have four children.